Contents

4	Acknowledgements
5	About the Author
6	Introduction
7	In The Field
12	Map Reading
15	Safe Storage
18	Identification & Assessment
27	Introduction to Cleaning Finds
32	Mechanical Cleaning
40	Electrolysis
45	Chemical Cleaning & Conservation
64	Repair, Restoration & Replication
78	Photographing Your Finds
86	Storage & Display
97	The Treasure Act
108	Bibliography and Suppliers

Editor Greg Payne

Design & Layout Sally Robinson

Published by Greenlight Publishing
The Publishing House, 119 Newland Street
Witham, Essex CM8 1WF
Tel: 01376 521900   **Fax:** 01376 521901
mail@greenlightpublishing.co.uk
www.greenlightpublishing.co.uk

Printed in Great Britain
ISBN 978 1 897738 337
© 2008 David Villanueva

All rights reserved. No part of this publication may be reproduced, stored in a retrieval system, or transmitted in any form by any means, electronic, mechanical photocopying, recording or otherwise, without the prior permission of Greenlight Publishing.

Acknowledgements

For invaluable help with this book I would like to thank:-

Alan Bradshaw
Brian Port
Gill Davies (with special thanks for proof reading the draft MS)
Janet Dove
John Hepburn
Kevin Reader
Ordnance Survey
Simon Harvey
W. Holden, Jewellers

Although discretion does not permit me to mention them by name, I would also like to thank my land-owning friends for generously allowing me to investigate their land and recover most of the metal objects discussed and shown in this book. This for me has brought local history to life as well as giving me the opportunity to practise my finds care skills.

I would also like to thank my many friends - inside and outside the metal detecting hobby - for their help, support and encouragement.

Finally I would like to dedicate this book to Helen.

About the Author

David Villanueva was born in Birmingham in 1951 and grew up in the Midlands. At school David's two main interests were history and science - particularly chemistry, where he made his mark on the laboratory wall when his rocket fuel project exploded. In spite of the set-back, David embarked on a technical career after leaving school, firstly as a medical laboratory technician and then on to quality control in the paper industry. This quickly led to various managerial positions, all with a technical bias.

In the early 1970s his mother bought him a copy of Ted Fletcher's book **A Fortune Under Your Feet**, which inspired him to buy a metal detector - a Goldfinger BFO. The performance was very poor by current standards but it did find coins and David became hooked. A few months later he upgraded to a deeper-seeking machine and became very fond of searching beaches, which were very productive of modern coins and jewellery at the time. In those early days David also took an interest in other forms of treasure hunting including dump digging, SCUBA diving, and gold panning.

Following a move to Whitstable in Kent, David took to nearby beaches with his trusty old Pulsedec, but quickly found that the machine was not well-suited to local conditions - the Pulsedec had no discrimination and there was plenty of iron around. He changed to a locally produced C-Scope 1220B, which worked well on the drier parts of the beaches, and this encouraged him to try out some inland sites.

He joined a metal detecting club and also gained permission to search a small farm, making all sorts of finds that previously he had only read about in **Treasure Hunting** magazine (hammered silver coins, for instance).

Having long had a keen interest in history David started researching his locality, which led to more productive sites to search and to write about in **Treasure Hunting**. The large quantities of metal objects he found gave him plenty of opportunity to hone his skills in conservation and cleaning over many years and, with his technical background, he is well qualified to explain how anyone can care for their finds safely.

Introduction

The removal of a metal object from the ground on one hand saves that object from the ravages of agricultural machinery, fertilisers or the sea but on the other triggers decay in most metals that could lead to total destruction unless some form of preservation or conservation is undertaken. Many argue that only professional conservators should carry out conservation; but in the real world there are thousands of objects being unearthed that would benefit from such treatment and few conservators available to do the work. In addition, the majority of metal detected finds have little value other than perhaps curiosity and interest - so who would be prepared to spend many times an object's worth to save it?

The transfer of finds from the ground to relatively safe storage (as will be explained) is a very easy, low cost operation, which incurs almost zero risk to personal safety and the find itself. Unfortunately, that method of dealing with the matter will not satisfy the majority who want to study or display their finds in some way or other. All finds of significant monetary or historical value are best either left alone or left to experts. However, unless you have very deep pockets to pay professionals to clean and conserve all your finds, the only way forward for low value finds of negligible historical importance is the "do-it-yourself" route. This opens up a whole new ball-game where you put both yourself and your find at risk of injury. All cleaning methods whether mechanical, electrical or chemical can be hazardous to your health and may result in the total destruction of your find. I will point out all the risks involved so that you can make informed decisions on which methods you can use. But it is entirely up to you and if you do not feel competent, or are in any doubt about taking the risks, then the best advice is *don't*.

Please remember:-

Do-it-yourself cleaning and conservation may seriously damage your health and your finds. The procedures within this book are provided in good faith and with recommended safety precautions. However, the author and publishers will accept no liability for accidents or damage resulting from the use of any materials or methods described.

Despite the above necessary warnings, with care, patience, and practice there is a great deal that almost anyone can do to conserve, clean and present their finds, using materials that are readily available and relatively safe to use. Read the following chapters carefully and then try a few experiments on your junk finds. Hopefully, you'll soon have good-looking finds and impressive displays.

In The Field

Having put the effort into making that nice find in the first place, the last thing you want to do is to damage it or lose it. You would also be wise to record the find spot, if for no other reason than your finds rate will improve if you can identify "hot spots" to return to. If you have been in the metal detecting hobby for any length of time you will already have some sort of system in place for gathering your finds and bringing them home safely. You may also have a find spot recording system. However, I may be able to improve on your system and can certainly show novices the way forward.

Taking care of your find starts while it is still in the ground. The first issue is extracting it from its resting place without damage - I can't imagine anything worse than having a nice find ruined by being hit with a digging tool. If your detector has a pinpoint mode it is advisable to use it to identify the position of your find in the ground as closely as possible before you start digging. Metal detectors vary on pinpoint accuracy and only experience will tell you how big a diameter hole you need to dig to avoid striking the find. Start with a generously large diameter and only reduce it as you gain experience over time.

An extremely useful accessory is an electronic pinpoint probe, a miniature metal detector, available from most metal detector dealers at around £30-£60. This gadget helps identify the exact position of the find in the hole so you can not only avoid damage but also speed up find extraction considerably. Bear in mind, though, that because of the probe's small size detection range is very limited, being no more than an inch on a small coin or artefact.

Pinpoint probe.

There are a few circumstances where you might not want to extract your find. Live ordnance or human remains should be left in the ground. Mark or record the spot and inform the landowner and the police. If you are lucky enough to discover a hoard or ritual deposit, you may need expert help and special equipment to get the find out of the ground intact. If you have a camera with you, photograph the find in the ground; then record the find spot, refill the hole, and contact your Finds Liaison Officer or local museum.

Having extracted the find you need somewhere to put it safely. You might have pockets but a failing pocket might have been responsible for the loss of the find in the first place. You really need a finds bag. The type I prefer is the apron type similar to those worn by market traders for holding their cash; they are again available from most metal detector retailers. Those I use have four deep pockets: the front two being open and the rear two zipped. Being right-handed I use the right front pocket for trash; the right rear pocket for sturdy finds; the left front pocket for my pinpoint probe; and the left rear pocket for polythene bags, marker, and to keep any fragile, important or easily damaged finds (each in its own bag). Of course, you need to take care not to pull out and lose any bagged finds when you pull out the next empty bag.

As you will gather from the previous paragraph, I take *all* of my finds home with me even if they appear to be total rubbish. Quite apart from not wanting to keep digging the same old junk up over and over again, I wouldn't want to throw away something interesting or valuable as several detectorists have done. I could relate several stories but this one should suffice. Dave (no, not me) kept finding small black rings and thinking they were curtain rings tossed each of them into a nearby hedge as he found them. At about the tenth one he decided to take a closer look and found a hallmark. They were gold wedding rings from London refuse that had been fire-blackened in the brick-making process. As you might imagine, Dave had great difficulty in re-locating those he had thrown away; in fact, so far as I know, most are still in the hedge somewhere. I go carefully through all my finds when I get home and keep everything that is interesting, or even remotely interesting. Of the remainder - consisting mainly of modern junk and shapeless pieces of metal unlikely to have any pedigree - I divide all non-ferrous metal I can into aluminium, copper alloy and lead to be sold for scrap. I put the rest - consisting generally of foil and modern iron - into containers for waste recycling.

Some finds from wet environments, such as beaches and foreshores, may have organic material like leather, textiles or wood attached, which will decay rapidly if dried out on exposure to air. Until you have the opportunity to determine what exactly you have, such types of find are best kept wet in a sealed plastic bag.

Finds bag.

There are many benefits to be gained from keeping track of find spots. Metal objects are mainly lost where human beings were active in the past, which creates "hot spots" that will yield numerous coins and artefacts relating to the period of activity. By logging your find spots you will see patterns emerging that will lead to more good finds and may add interest to your searches as the picture of past human activity develops. Most landowners are intensely interested in the finds from their land and like to know at least what was found, where it was found, and why it was there in the first place. By answering as many of their questions as you can, you will endear yourself to the landowner with obvious benefits.

If your find happens to be classed as potential Treasure then there is a requirement to supply an accurate find spot. While this is not strictly mandatory, the Treasure Act Code of Practice does imply that awards could be abated for failing to identify the find spot. The Portable Antiquities Scheme has set up a network of Finds Liaison Officers and a database for recording finds (mainly over 300 years old) made by the public. Reporting is entirely voluntary and must be with the landowner's permission. However, I feel we should report finds to the PAS if we possibly can - it is good for the hobby in that we are giving information back for what we are taking away.

Many detectorists seem to have developed a photographic memory so far as memorising where objects were found. If you have such a memory then perhaps you need do nothing more than record your finds on a map, in a notebook, or on a database when you get home from detecting. When your memory starts to fail, and for the less fortunate, probably the best way to record finds in the field is to place significant finds in numbered polythene bags cross-referenced to a map or Global Positioning System. At this stage you can use any small polythene bags between about 7.5cm (3 inches) square to about 20cm (8 inches) square that can be closed to prevent the find falling out. You can get small sealable polythene bags from most stationers or supermarkets for finds that don't need to be kept wet. The polythene bags need to be numbered with a suitable permanent marker which you can do before you go out detecting or take the marker with you and number the bags as you make the finds. Permanent markers with bullet points are easier to write with than the alternative chisel points.

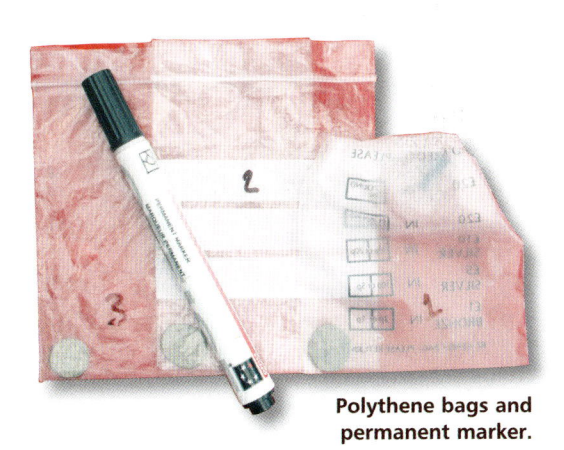

Polythene bags and permanent marker.

I don't suppose you really want to carry large maps around with you in the field; however, a cheap and effective alternative is to use a credit card wallet and make copies of maps or sketches of the fields you are searching on cards which you keep in the wallet. When you make a significant find you pop it in a numbered bag and use a fine tipped permanent marker to mark the find spot on the map card.

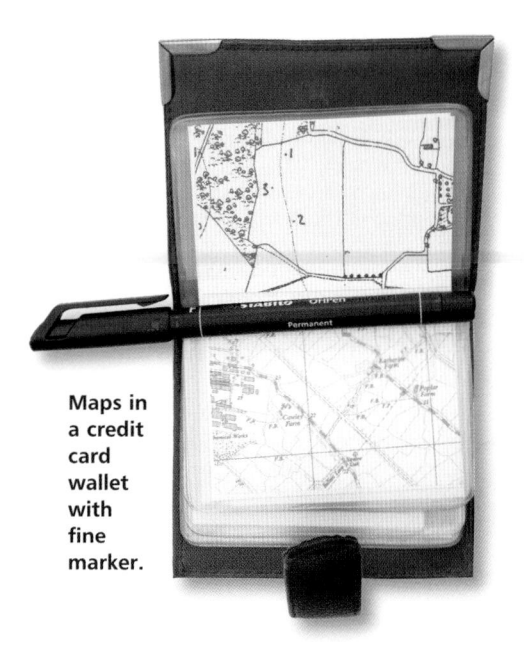

Maps in a credit card wallet with fine marker.

The highly technical method of find spot recording is to use a hand-held Global Positioning System (GPS). In the 1970s the United States Defense Department developed GPS so that military units would know their own and other units exact location anywhere on the planet. The system works by means of 24 satellites orbiting the earth and arranged so that at least six satellites are transmitting their position and time data to any point in the world. Portable or hand-held receivers collect the satellite data and determine the instrument's exact location, elevation, speed and time, 24 hours a day

regardless of the weather. GPS is being increasingly used in cars, boats and planes, where it is more usually called satellite navigation or "satnav" and is free for anyone to use. You just have to buy a receiver, which are now fairly modestly priced and not much bigger than a mobile phone.

You may have heard that the public GPS receivers are deliberately inaccurate. That was the case until May 2000 when "Selective Availability", the satellite signal error, was switched off. Now GPS is almost unbelievably accurate to within a metre or two, which is extremely useful for plotting find spots - especially as the receiver can determine location by Ordnance Survey grid reference.

I have recently updated my own GPS receiver from a fairly ancient Magellan GPS 2000 to a smaller, neater, faster satellite finding Garmin eTrex H. Using this I'll describe how to record a find spot. It is very simple. First switch on and wait a minute or two for the receiver to lock on to the satellites (which you would normally do at the beginning of your detecting session). When you have dug a find you want to log, you stand on the find spot and toggle through the pages to the menu page. Enter "mark". The next sequential number is displayed with the Grid Reference and "OK?" Enter again and the find spot is logged until you delete it. To recall the find spot you toggle through the pages to the menu page. Enter "waypoints". The list is displayed which you toggle through to the find spot you want and read it off for recording on your map or database (or you can navigate your way back to it). The Garmin eTrex H can store up to

500 find spots, which it will retain until you delete them regardless of the device being switched on or off.

While it is not considered good practice to wash or clean a find in the field, I do carry some basic washing equipment with me on my forays that I leave in the car. The reason for this is that although I have the will-power to wait until I get home before doing anything with a find, on a couple of occasions I have found potential Treasure, which I have needed to show to the landowner and his family on the spot. There is a great temptation here for people to try and rub the dirt off, which could do great damage to the object, particularly if it is gold. It is much better to carefully wash the find before allowing it to be handled by others. So my washing kit consists of a travel dog bowl with integral water supply (from a pet shop), a soft toothbrush, and a small plastic sieve or tea strainer to hold the find and catch anything important that might be washed off.

GPS find spot marked at OS TR14979 57865.

Portable washing kit (two alternative versions of bowl shown).

11

Map Reading

Even if you're using GPS to record find spots you will probably want to plot them on a map to see patterns emerging and perhaps as a permanent record. If you don't have GPS then you will need some basic map reading skills to record your find spots anyway. So it is worthwhile knowing how to use the National Grid unique reference system, which can be applied to all modern Ordnance Survey maps regardless of the scale.

The National Grid Reference System (NGR)

Under the current National Grid System, Great Britain (England, Scotland and Wales) is overlaid with a square grid made up of twenty-five 500 kilometre squares, each given a letter from A through to Z (omitting I) starting from the north-west corner and ending at the south-east corner. This grid is so large that the "A" square is somewhere around Iceland and the "Z" square in continental Europe. Only four of these squares cover land in Britain: "H", "N", "S" and "T" which form the first letter of the grid reference.

The 500km squares are then divided up into twenty-five 100 kilometre squares, using the same lettering system, which gives the second letter of the grid reference. Also there is a numbering system, which starts with zero at the south-west corner of the "S" 500 kilometre square, south-west of the Scilly Isles. So each of the 100 kilometre squares are numbered, at their south-west corners: 0, 100, 200, …600, along the horizontal axis, west to east and 0, 100, 200, …1200, along the vertical axis, south to north. Each of the 100 kilometre squares is further divided by gridlines into ten 10 kilometre squares. Each of the 10 kilometre squares is sub-divided by lighter gridlines into ten 1 kilometre squares.

To determine the grid reference, read the horizontal axis (called Eastings) first followed by the vertical axis (called Northings). There is a little phrase to help remember this: "Along the corridor, then up the stairs".

The very first number, called the co-ordinate reference, is small and identifies the 100 kilometre square. On modern OS maps the co-ordinate numbers are printed in front of the gridline numbers on the four corner grids. The usual practice is to ignore this number for both Eastings and Northings and replace it with the grid or area letters which, depending on the map, can be found in the corners of the map (*Landranger*), in the legend (*Explorer*), or on the cover (*Pathfinder*). However, this number is used to give map references in some instances. The second number represents the 10 kilometre grid and the third number the 1 kilometre grid. After this it is not too difficult to estimate the number of tenths within the grid to give a closer reference to within 100 metres on the ground (a six-figure reference). With a larger scale map the number of tenths can be estimated again to give a reference within 10 metres on the ground (an eight-figure reference).

The accuracy of these references can be greatly improved with a handy little device called Where-Wolf, which is a small plastic card engraved with a grid. The grid is designed to overlay the 1 kilometre grid on Ordnance Survey 1.25 inch to 1 mile *Landranger* maps and all 2.5 inch to 1 mile maps such as the *Explorer* and *Pathfinder*. It is then very easy to read off the find spot.

So let's have a look at a real map, Sheet 31/57. This is the south-west corner of an Ordnance Survey 2.5 inch to 1 mile map published 1953 and is now part of the ST area. Okay, let's find the reference for "Ancient Earthwork" (above Flailand) three squares east and two north from the corner. The NGR reference starts with the two letters: ST, then we look along the horizontal grid numbers for the number on the grid line immediately to the west of Ancient Earthwork, 52; then measure or estimate the number of tenths east of the "52" gridline, which is 0. So, the first part of the reference is ST520. Now all we do is repeat the procedure for the vertical grid numbers using the grid line immediately to the south of Ancient Earthwork, so that gives us 71 plus 9 for the tenths north of the "71" gridline. So the full 6 figure NGR is ST520719. If we use Where-Wolf on top of the 52/71 square we can not only confirm that our reference is correct but can easily work out the 8 figure NGR which is ST52037193.

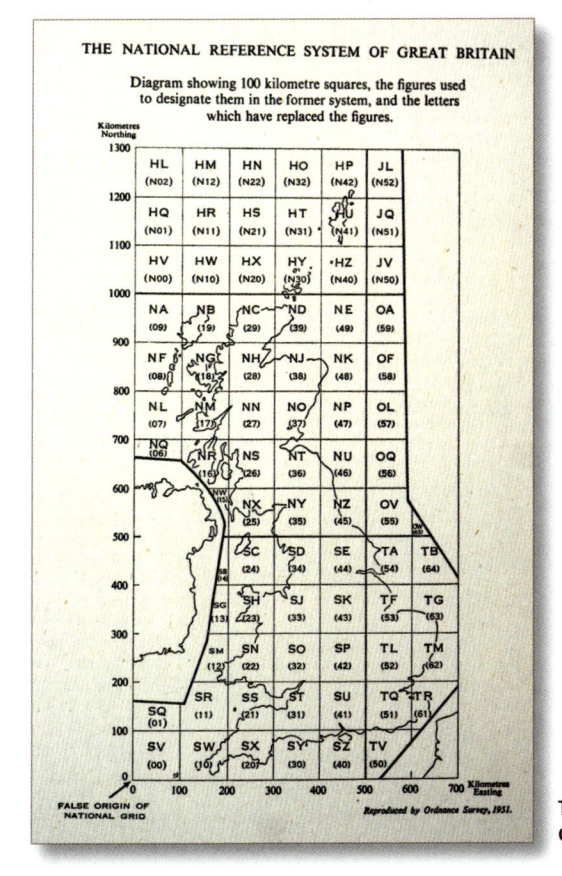

The Ordnance Survey National Grid Reference System.

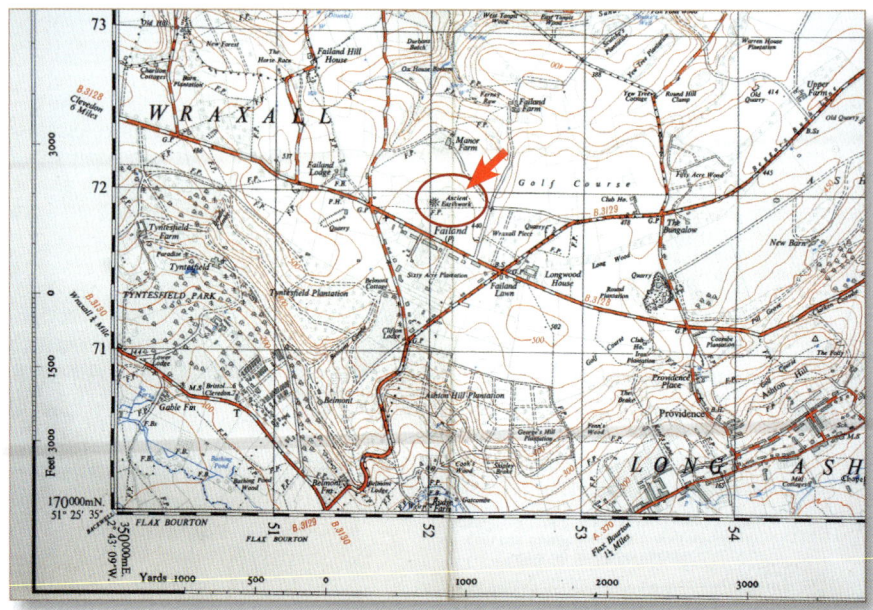

OS Sheet 31/57, 1953.

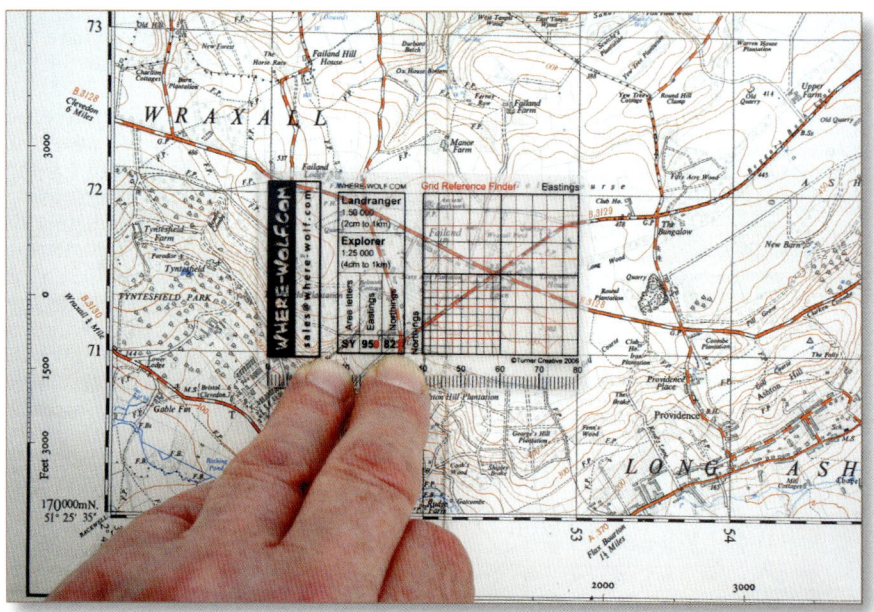

Using Where-Wolf.

14

Safe Storage

There are two agents necessary for the corrosion of metals to take place - moisture and oxygen. If we can eliminate one or the other then we can effectively stop any further corrosion taking place. A classic school experiment demonstrates that iron nails will not rust if kept in water where the dissolved oxygen has been removed by boiling. That particular science lesson does not lend itself to a practical storage method for most finds but fortunately the reduction or elimination of moisture does.

The measurement of the percentage of moisture content in air is called Relative Humidity (RH): 0% RH is bone dry; 100% RH is saturated. The ambient or normal humidity inside most buildings will usually be 50% RH with a variance of 10% either way. According to studies, copper alloys will not corrode below 35% RH, nor will iron kept below 15% RH.

For several decades conservationists have advocated using a "Dry Box" to store metal finds, providing there is no organic material attached. This method certainly deserves consideration even if it is only used as a short-term measure to keep finds stable until you have the time and inclination to prepare them for alternative storage or display.

The Portable Antiquities Scheme (PAS) have devised a recommended Dry Box kit consisting of a large (7.5 litre) airtight polythene box, 6 x 100 grams silica gel bags, a humidity indicator card, a quantity of grip-top write-on bags; sizes 85mm (3.5 inch) x 114mm (4.5 inch) and 191mm (7.5 inch) square (some filled with 4mm jiffy foam), a permanent marker, a pair of powder-free nitrile gloves and 15 spun bonded polythene "Tyvek" labels approximately 85mm (3.5 inch) x 50mm (2 inch). At the time of writing at least two metal detector retailers are offering Dry Boxes based on the above and more will probably follow suit. Buying a ready-made kit is the easiest way to get started; however, suppliers of the various components are given at the end of this book.

So what do you do with all this? The basic Dry Box is the airtight plastic box containing approximately 100 grams of silica gel per litre of box, which will absorb moisture from the air in the box and maintain a dry environment until the silica gel becomes saturated. The indicator strip, which should be taped to the inside of the box facing outwards and kept away from strong sunlight, monitors the RH in the box; the blue panels turning progressively pink as the silica gel absorbs moisture and loses efficiency. When the RH reaches 30% (10% if you are storing iron) the silica gel needs to be dried out, which is fairly simply achieved in an oven on very slow heat 110-120° C; (225-250° F; gas mark quarter to half)

15

for up to several hours to evaporate off the moisture. If you are using a gas oven be careful not to set fire to the bags containing the silica gel. After one hour, weigh the silica gel bags on your kitchen scales and note the weight, then return them to the oven for a further hour and reweigh. If there is no loss in weight then the bags are completely dry and can be returned to the dry box, if there is weight loss, note the weight and return them to the oven for a further hour. Repeat the process until there is no further weight loss. The box should stay "dry" for several months before the silica gel needs drying out but remember that every time you take the lid off the box damp air will flood in and shorten the period.

Keep all the other materials separate from the Dry Box until you need to add a find to the box. You will need to be selective as to what finds you put in the box otherwise you will rapidly fill the box. Firstly there will be the occasional find with organic material attached which will probably need keeping wet and secondly there is little point in keeping gold in your Dry Box as it doesn't corrode. I would suggest that most modern finds of less than say 300 years old won't be in imminent danger of corroding away to dust (iron excepted) and can be kept quite happily for long periods in approximately half litre (500ml) size labelled plastic boxes with lids. These boxes can be bought very cheaply from "pound shops" or salvaged from your Chinese take-away meal. Have a look at the contents of these boxes every couple of months or so and if anything is showing signs of deteriorating then re-assign it to your Dry Box. Fragile finds should still be stored in protective packaging within the plastic box or confined to the Dry Box.

The conservationists say that all you should do to your finds is to let them dry out at room temperature (not on radiators or in ovens as they may shatter) on white kitchen towel, unwashed, and then put them in the Dry Box. This is because washing can cause further corrosion and damage or lose fragile plating, inlay or associated organic material. Most detecting finds are fairly robust and having made an initial assessment, I prefer to carefully wash my finds so I know what I am dealing with. I don't believe one more soaking will do any harm to something that has lain in damp ground for aeons and there will be slightly less volume to keep dry.

You then need to put your find in a perforated grip-top polythene bag, filled with 4mm Jiffy foam or around 10 sheets of acid-free tissue paper to cushion it and label the bag with a permanent marker. Grip-top polythene bags are normally supplied un-perforated so to perforate your empty bag you can use a standard two-hole paper punch and punch it once on each of the two vertical edges of the bag, which will add eight holes in total. You will find it much easier to punch the holes if you slide a piece of scrap thin card in the punch underneath and supporting the bag. Write the find details on the bag, slide the Jiffy foam or acid-free tissue in, followed by the find, seal the gripper so your find doesn't fall out, add the complete package to your Dry Box, and replace the lid securely. All you need to do then is to keep an eye on the RH indicator now and again and check your finds over when you have to dry out the silica gel.

Dry Box (lid removed to show contents).

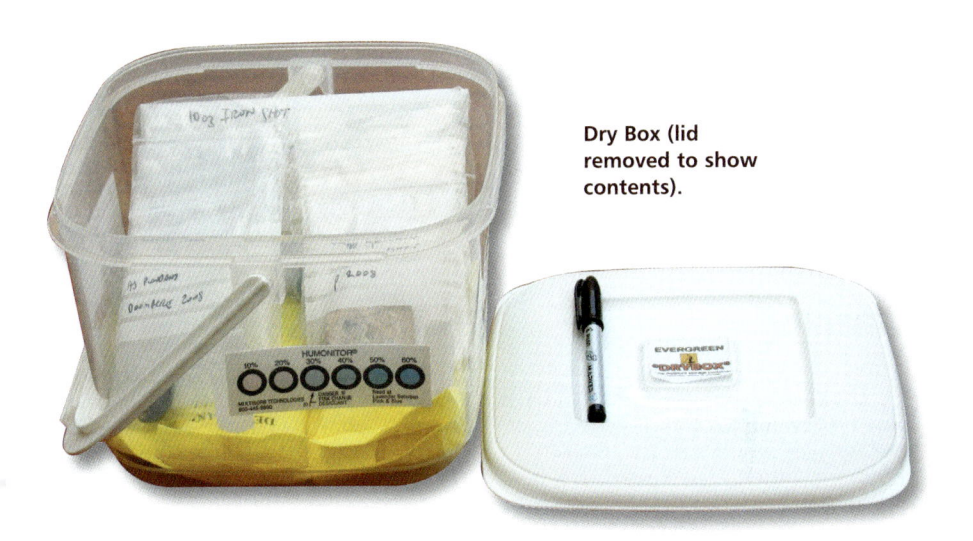

On the rare occasion that you have a metal find with organic material attached, the best way of preserving it in the short term is to keep it in a Wet Box. Ideally this should be a clear plastic box with an airtight lid like the Dry Box. It is easier to keep objects wet than dry so most plastic food containers will suffice. Simply place the find in a labelled perforated bag without the Jiffy foam or acid-free tissue and keep it covered in reasonably pure water. If the material floats, weigh it down with some inert material like pebbles. Change the water fortnightly to discourage bacterial growth and algae. Unfortunately, conservation of organic materials is a specialist job that cannot really be done at home, so you will need to seek advice from your Finds Liaison Officer or local museum on the best way of preserving your find.

Identification & Assessment

Washing

The majority of your finds will have varying amounts of dirt adhering to the surfaces and if you are going to do anything, other than keep them in a Dry Box for posterity you will need to at least wash them. Washing, as opposed to cleaning, means rinsing with water and can include gentle removal of dirt, in water, with a soft toothbrush.

Let's start with water quality. In principle all substances that you use on your finds should be as pure as reasonably practicable to prevent undesirable effects or damage and give consistently good results. Water quality is important too. For the sake of argument, I will use the term pure water throughout this book to mean the best quality available. The purest water you can get is distilled water, which is water that has been boiled to turn it to steam, and then condensed back to water. It is not melted ice from the freezer, which is no better than tap water. Also it would not be very sensible to try and produce distilled water at home using a kettle. Distilled water may be available in bottles at some supermarkets, garages and ironmongers as it has traditionally been used for topping-up car batteries and steam irons but it is becoming increasingly rare.

The next best grade is de-ionised water, which is water that has been passed through an ion-exchange filter, which renders impurities more soluble and relatively harmless. De-ionised water is relatively cheap and readily available in bottles at supermarkets and garages etc. but avoid the fashionable scented water for steam irons. You can easily produce de-ionised water at home in almost unlimited quantities by using a jug or tap filter of the Brita type, which is what I use. They're your finds and if you don't want to use de-ionised water, cooled boiled tap water, which leaves some impurities behind in the kettle is the next best quality followed by tap water itself. Using mineral water, river water, water from muddy puddles or seawater is best avoided.

Having said all that, if your find is covered in dirt rinsing it will rapidly contaminate even the purest water and you may as well do most of the washing with tap water. But do not wash your find directly under the tap. When your find is covered in dirt and/or corrosion you probably won't be able to see things that are about to fall off. How would you feel if you washed away a valuable precious stone from a nice piece of jewellery? That's probably the worst nightmare but nevertheless something to bear in mind. It is safest to always wash finds individually and to gently apply water from a wash bottle over a small bowl or sieve initially, until you are sure that a more thorough wash won't do any harm.

There are two ways to wash finds, which would avoid losing anything that detaches from them. The first is to use a small plastic bowl and wash the find gently in that by swishing it around, changing the water when it gets cloudy, and at the same time taking care not to throw out anything with the dirty water. A soft toothbrush can be used if necessary, but be aware that scrubbing may remove plating, inlays and even surface detail. The second method is to wash the find in a suitable culinary plastic sieve, which come in various sizes from tea strainer to flour sieve. The find is placed in the sieve, which is then placed in a bowl of water. Moving the sieve gently from side to side will wash the find but anything falling off will be retained in the sieve. Again a soft toothbrush can be used but keep the find within the confines of the mesh. Whichever method you use it would be best to perform a final rinse of the find over the bowl or sieve using the purest water available applied from a wash bottle. Laboratory wash bottles are best but a plastic soft drinks bottle with either a "sports" or sprinkler top will do the job.

Wash bottles, sieves and bowls.

Identification of Metals

Aluminium: a soft, light, white metal not produced commercially until 1854 so finds won't be very old. May be shiny or have a grey tarnish or white corrosion.

Aluminium button.

Copper and alloys: copper and bronze (copper-tin alloy) are a red-brown colour; brass (copper-zinc alloy) is yellow; cupronickel (copper-nickel alloy) and nickel silver (copper-zinc-nickel alloy) are both silver or white coloured. Excavated copper-alloys are usually smooth green or black (may be patchy with bare metal) or powdery green.

Copper-alloy coins.

Gold: a soft, heavy, yellow metal, which usually comes out of the ground bright and shiny. Gold alloys may show green (copper) or purple (silver) spots or hue. In modern jewellery gold is often specially alloyed to produce other colours such as white or rose (red).

A 9 carat gold signet ring.

Iron and steel: a grey, magnetic metal that is usually found covered in lumpy orange rust (except stainless steel, which usually remains bright and shiny). Test with a magnet and if the magnet sticks, the metal is (or contains) iron or steel.

A 10oz iron cannonball.

20

Lead: a soft, heavy, grey metal often excavated with a white or grey surface coating. Lead is a poison, which can be absorbed through human skin so handle with waterproof gloves.

Engraved lead object.

CM

Pewter spoon handle.

Nickel: a hard silvery-white metal discovered in 1751. Pure nickel is used for specialist tools and equipment such as medical and laboratory ware, otherwise it is usually found alloyed with copper and other metals as either a modern coining metal or tableware. Cupro-nickel coins often have a red colour as a result of the copper leaching out.

CM

Cupro-nickel coin.

Pewter: a white to grey alloy of lead and tin. Excavated pewter is usually dark grey, may be flaky and may have a white to grey surface coating.

Platinum: a white, heavy shiny metal mostly used in fairly modern jewellery (discovered in 1735).

Silver: a white metal, which may come out of the ground bright and shiny or have a smooth black tarnish, or white, grey, lilac or green (when alloyed with copper) corrosion. May be very brittle and easily cracked. Oils and salts in the skin attack silver so it is best handled wearing cotton or waterproof gloves.

Silver Victoria shilling.

Silver medallion.

CM

Silver medieval coin.

21

Tin: a white metal, which usually has a dull earthy surface when excavated, usually found as a protective coating on iron or steel.

Charles II tin farthing.

Zinc: a dull grey metal usually excavated as bare metal but may have white powdery spots, often in deep pits. Although used by the Romans alloyed with copper for coinage, most zinc finds will be relatively modern.

Die-cast zinc model car. The roof has been stripped to show bare metal.

There are also a few unusual metals such as titanium and palladium that are mainly used in modern jewellery, so if you find anything that doesn't fit into the above I'm afraid you'll have to seek out specialist advice. If the object is jewellery then your local independent jeweller will probably be able to help.

Palladium finger ring.

Gold & Silver Testing

Before you start with any testing, look closely at the object, with a good quality magnifier, if necessary. All modern gold, silver and platinum (since 1975) artefacts in the UK, whether made here or imported and containing over 7.8 gram silver or 1 gram gold or 0.5 gram platinum, should be hallmarked. A good little book on hallmarks is: **English Silver Hall-marks** by Judith Banister (London, 1970-2004). Although the title reads "silver" it covers gold and platinum as well.

Another tool that you will find useful for identification as well as for making up chemical solutions is an accurate weighing device. A jeweller's scales in a portable boxed set with weights is readily available for around £5 either new or second-hand. The weighing range is 10 milligrams (.01 gram) to 20 grams. There are no batteries and little to go wrong with this one other than losing the weights.

Less fiddly, although more expensive, are pocket-size digital scales but most of them are quite delicate and won't survive dropping or soaking. A range of around 0.1 gram to 50 or 100 gram will be ideal for our purposes. These balances are also useful for identifying gold and silver coins both British and foreign, where the issued weight is usually given in coin catalogues. Coins are traditionally weighed in grains and pan weights do exist for this purpose, although they would not be easy to get hold of unless you can find or make your own. You can now buy one mini digital scale that can weigh in virtually all units: grams, ounces, troy ounces, pennyweights, grains and carats but they aren't particularly cheap. An alternative is to weigh in grams and use a calculator to convert to the other units you might require.

Traditional and digital weighing devices.

1 grain = 0.0648 grams (g)	1 gram = 15.432 grains (gn)
1 pennyweight (24 grains) = 1.5552 grams	1 gram = 0.643 pennyweight (dwt)
1 troy ounce (20 pennyweights) = 31.1035 grams	1 gram = 0.03215 troy ounce (ozt)
1 ounce avoirdupois or imperial = 28.35 grams	1 gram = 0.03527 ounces (oz)

Before we get to the acid test the first thing to try is a magnet. Precious metals are not magnetic but some "silver" artefacts may turn out to be stainless steel, which, although less magnetic than iron, is attracted to a strong magnet. Nothing so far discussed will damage your find; but the acid test will. It is not only a destructive test but also uses strong inorganic acids, which can destroy clothes and flesh if you are careless with them, so only use the acid test as a last resort.

If your find could be over 300 years old and fall within the remit of the Treasure Act then do not use the acid test; report the object as possible Treasure. If you are not told by the FLO or museum curator that it definitely isn't Treasure, then the British Museum, which receives the find, has non-destructive X-ray analysis equipment, that can determine the precious metal content precisely without inflicting any damage to the find whatsoever. What's more there is no charge for this service, even if the object is disclaimed.

For modern, possible precious metal finds, you could use the expertise and equipment of your local independent jeweller whom, I am sure, will test the object for you for a modest fee. On the other hand if you are finding quantities of modern potentially precious metal objects, you might want to get your own testing kit. These kits are available from some metal detector dealers and jewellery trade suppliers and vary in price and versatility from simple gold/not gold and silver/not silver to identifying the percentage of gold (9 carat, 14 carat, 18 carat, 22 carat) and testing for platinum also. I wouldn't bother paying extra for platinum testing as the metal is rarely found and the test is negative anyway (or in other words if there is no response to the test the object is probably platinum).

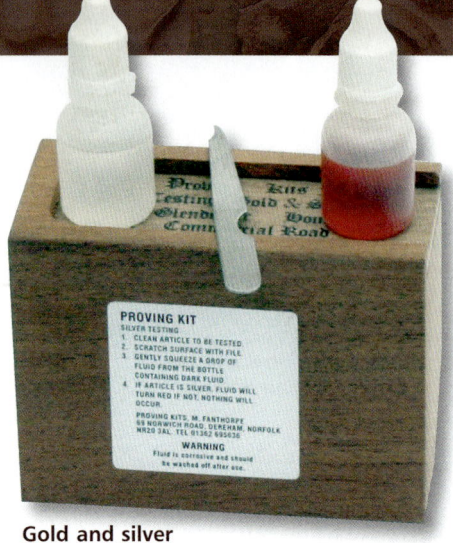

Gold and silver test (proving) kit.

Wearing vinyl (PVC) gloves and eye protection, place a tiny spot of acid on the filed area of the object via the applicator built into the bottle cap. The acid will change colour, indicating whether the object is gold or silver and also indicate the purity (depending on the kit). You must thoroughly wash off the acid or it will continue to attack the object. You should then be able to improve or remove the marks left from the test by polishing with a soft cloth and jewellers' rouge.

The Acid Test

(Please read the chapter on health and safety on page 27 before attempting any of the methods described below.)

You will need a steady hand for this and reasonable eyesight although colour-blindness shouldn't be a problem. Also, keep a bottle of alkaline solution handy as an instant neutraliser in case you get acid on your skin or clothes. Strong acids burn! Suitable alkalis include ammonia, sodium bicarbonate, and sodium carbonate solutions.

Before testing the object you will have to file the surface with a fine steel needle file or nail file to get through any plating. If the object is gold plated the surface will be gold and will test positive for gold; likewise silver plating will test positive for silver. A small file is usually included with the test kit and needle files are available from jeweller's suppliers and many shops selling tools. Select a place on the object that is not normally seen and file the surface firmly but only over a very small area.

Identification

Before you start any form of cleaning you really need to try and identify the object and have some idea of its historic and monetary value. Coin collectors and dealers will probably tell you that a coin can be reduced to a tenth of its monetary value by cleaning, although you rarely see coins for sale covered in muck and corrosion unless they are being sold specifically as uncleaned.

Sometimes it can be a Catch 22 situation where an object has little value because it cannot be identified for lack of cleaning; but cleaning reduces the value to a fraction of what it would have been if it hadn't been cleaned in the first place. However, it is a good idea to try and identify and value everything before you start cleaning and you'll know what you stand to lose if it goes wrong or whether it is worthwhile paying for a professional conservator to carry out the task. Potential Treasure objects are not a problem. Do not clean them: just report them and hand them in and if they are disclaimed and returned to you, you can deal with them then with the benefit of a clear identification.

Coins are fairly easy to identify and value from catalogues; even an old catalogue is useful and will give a relative value. **Coins of England & the United Kingdom** (Spink, published annually), is the main British catalogue. There are world coin catalogues, and catalogues covering many foreign countries - providing you can identify which country issued the coin in the first place.

I only know of one general catalogue of artefacts which is **Benet's Artefacts of England & the United Kingdom** (Greenlight Publishing, 2003). This is beautifully illustrated with colour photographs of high quality artefacts. If your find is in Benet's then you will know you have arrived! You will also know the value and can proceed accordingly. Greenlight Publishing produce a wide range of books on identifying finds, many with valuations (an illustrated list will be found at the back of this book). Many detectorists build their own library of reference books for identification, but if you are just starting out you could try the public library.

Your Finds Liaison Officer or local museum curator can usually assist in finds identification and relative scarcity rather than valuation. They won't be expert in all types of metal object, although they can usually find a specialist in the type of object you show them. Most FLOs hold finds identification days.

The Portable Antiquities Scheme (PAS) www.finds.org.uk has a large database of finds: over a third of a million objects have been recorded at time of writing. It will help with identification but not valuation. There is a facility, however, to search the *Treasure Annual Reports*, which record values where the objects have been declared Treasure and the annual reports themselves can be downloaded as pdf files (Adobe Acrobat) from: www.culture.gov.uk/Reference_library/Publications/

The PAS is such a major resource that I'll just comment on a few of its features. The Finds link on the navigation panel on the left hand side of the home page gives quick access to the Celtic Coin Index, and guides to identifying Roman, early-medieval and medieval coins. If you click on the Database box at the top of the home page you will get a screen with a choice of searches: quick or advanced. Quicksearch is the easiest way to search the database but does return a large number of results; however, there is a filter facility to refine the search. Advanced Search firstly allows you to select finds, coins, publications or images and then allows you to select to return only objects with images linked. There are then three boxes displayed. From the left drop-down box select the field to search such as object type, broad period, etc. From the middle drop-down box select the type of search such as the field "contains" or "is exactly" etc. In the right box type in the search term or better still use the list facility and select a term already in the database. You can then click on the "more" button to bring up a further set of boxes to enter another set of parameters to combine with the previous set. You can combine more search terms indefinitely by repeating the last operation.

There are help pages available. However, as an example I searched for a Roman silver finger ring with a gold stud as follows:

Object Type	Contains	finger ring
and		
Broad period	Contains	ROMAN
and		
Primary Material	is exactly	Silver
and		
Object Description	Contains	gold

This returned just two records for me to look at which included the ring I was looking for. By comparison, the Quicksearch only allows a search of the database summary and the best I could do was to search for Roman finger ring which returned 851 records.

The UK Detector Finds Database can be searched at www.ukdfd.co.uk although again there are no valuations. UK Detector Net www.forum ukdetectornet.co.uk hosts the largest British metal detecting forum on the Internet, which also has a finds identifying section and you should be able to obtain a valuation too.

Many small metal objects are offered for sale on Ebay (www.ebay.co.uk) so you can search completed listings to see what prices were achieved. If you know what an object basically is, you can search for information in a search engine such as Google (www.google.co.uk).

Introduction to Cleaning Finds

Corrosion of Metals

Few metals are found in their pure state naturally; even gold is usually found alloyed with silver and copper. Base metals are almost invariably found as minerals, which are metals compounded with non-metallic elements in a very stable form. Not surprisingly, metals buried in the ground for long periods tend to revert to their mineral form. Generally the less energy required to convert the mineral into its metal, the more stable is the metal. Little energy is required to convert the oxide cassiterite into tin, which re-oxidises much more slowly than copper and iron. For this reason tin has been used as a protective coating for the past 2,000 years, firstly on copper vessels and more recently on steel cans.

The more acid the soil, the greater its porosity, and the more soluble chemicals or salts are present, the faster buried metals corrode in the ground. The salts dissolve in moist earth to form electrolytes, which conduct electricity and will corrode most metals present by electrochemistry. This is why seawater, which contains relatively large amounts of salts, is so corrosive to most metals.

Buried metals that have already endured some corrosion have a relatively porous surface and are prone to retain small amounts of salts, often sealed by apparently stable encrustation. However, exposure to air and moisture often stimulates fresh corrosive activity that may result in surface pitting and, in the worse case, total disintegration. On the other hand, where corrosion has developed slowly and uniformly, a patina forms. This not only protects the object from further corrosion but may also enhance its appearance and value. Evenly patinated metal objects are best left alone as any cleaning can only reduce value and spoil appearance; however, if there is a clear need to treat such objects one should always endeavour to preserve the patina.

It is not necessary for metal objects to be buried for corrosion to take place, for even indoors moisture laden air will cause a dull film of surface oxidation, while industrial atmospheres carrying sulphurous gases cause dark sulphide coatings called tarnish. These effects are comparatively minor and respond readily to treatment.

There are three possible treatments to combat corrosion: mechanical, chemical and electrolytic. In many cases it is necessary to use more than one method, or even all three, to get the best possible results. The task now is to study all the methods then use your skill and judgement to visualise the finished object and decide how to stabilise your finds with the minimum of change necessary to achieve the desired result. Practice on junk finds first, it gets easier with practice.

Health & Safety

The majority of tools and substances discussed are relatively common domestic objects and no more hazardous in themselves than most tools and substances found in the home. However, a big difference here is the *special application* and it is essential that you are aware of the dangers that this application creates. For instance you eat small quantities of sodium bicarbonate in cakes and it is also a traditional indigestion remedy, but when used in the treatment of silver as described later it gives off a poisonous inflammable gas.

Specific hazards will be discussed later alongside specific cleaning techniques so I am only going to discuss generalities and types of protection here.

Accidents: If you do not have a water tap in the working area keep a bucket or bowl of fresh clean water handy and also an eye bath. Nearly all the chemicals in this book will be relatively harmless when spilt on the skin but it is good practice to quickly wash the affected part off with plenty of water. Your eyes are very sensitive and any substance getting into them other than pure water is likely to cause irritation so wash them immediately under a running tap or with an eye bath or wash bottle (sports or sprinkler top,

preferably). It is also a good idea to keep a First Aid kit nearby.

Apron: On the rare occasion that you may work with corrosive substances a PVC apron will protect much of your body and clothes. You can buy reusable or disposable industrial aprons or a plastic (not cloth) domestic apron would suffice.

Children and pets: should be kept away from the work area and all chemicals and tools should be kept out of reach or locked away.

Disposal: Chemical waste should not be poured down sinks and drains. Collect used solutions separately from each other (mixing may be dangerous) in suitably labelled containers and store out of reach of children and pets. Used plastic milk containers, washed out, are ideal for this purpose. Label the containers: "Used (name of chemical) Solution" with permanent marker. Take the filled containers to your household waste site for disposal.

Drinking, eating and smoking: Basically, don't drink, eat or smoke while cleaning or working with finds. Lead itself, and the corrosion products of some other metals, are toxic. Electrolysis and silver cleaning both generate inflammable gases. Most solvents are inflammable and some become very toxic when heated by a lighted cigarette, so smoking can seriously damage your health faster than you may think.

A dust mask should be worn during manual cleaning using hand tools where potentially toxic or irritating particles are being dislodged into the air (eg glass fibre or wire brushing, scalpel, picks). Suppliers of suitable dust masks include DIY stores, decorating suppliers, and hardware stores.

Dust mask.

Electricity: The great hazard here is using electrical devices with water or aqueous (water based) solutions, which definitely do not mix. Apparently several people die each year through watering the Christmas tree while the fairy lights are on! Electrical devices not treated with respect can be fatal!

Firstly the electricity supply. Do you have a fuse board or a consumer unit? A consumer unit houses miniature contact breakers (MCBs) which are wired into the live side of various mains circuits and trip to shut off electrical supply almost instantaneously on overload to protect against getting a major electric shock. The main switch is usually a Residual Current Detector (RCD), wired into both the live and neutral circuits. This analyses for current imbalance and also trips on overload, but is more sensitive than an MCB. If your mains supply is via a fuse board you really should use an RCD adapter (available from electrical and DIY stores), which plugs into any electrical socket and provides protection against electrocution. You can run all your electrical devices simultaneously from one RCD socket by plugging in a multi-way socket outlet. Even if you have a consumer unit it may be worth having the added protection of an RCD adapter, and the convenience of not tripping the main switch if anything goes wrong. Ensure that your hands are dry when plugging electrical equipment in or switching it on and off.

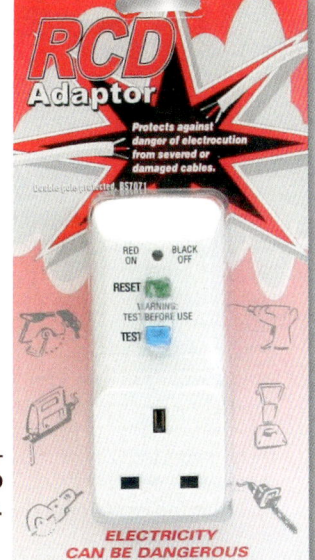

Plug-in RCD adaptor.

Eye protection: Murphy's law says that if anything, liquid or solid, flies into your face it will go in your eye. Harold II didn't live to tell the tale! So always use eye protection when you're handling any chemicals or doing any manual cleaning that creates dust or dislodges solid particles. Safety glasses are probably more comfortable than goggles but both are available from DIY stores and specialist safety suppliers. The best safety glasses to use are either wrap around or have side and brow guards. If you wear spectacles get the type that go over spectacles (spectacles alone won't give full eye protection unless you fit clip-on side guards).

der carries the latex into the air, which will affect those around you, even if you are not allergic yourself. So vinyl (PVC) or nitrile gloves are generally preferable. It is advisable to use gloves when handling finds, particularly silver (and photographs), as acids and oils in your skin can leave unsightly marks. Surgical gloves are also fine for this purpose or you may prefer cotton/fabric gloves as used in photography and catering (for this job only), as cotton gloves will not protect you from chemicals and the like. Surgical and cotton gloves are available from chemists and stationers.

Safety glasses.

Gloves: Wear waterproof gloves when you are handling chemicals, lead and during manual cleaning. While you can use household gloves of the "Marigold" type, disposable surgical type gloves tend to hug your hands and fingers like a second skin and allow you more control of whatever you are handling. Latex gloves hug more closely than other types; however, many people are allergic to them, suffering symptoms not unlike hay fever. The powder (corn starch) coated ones are the worst offenders as the pow-

Cotton and vinyl (PVC) gloves.

Naked flames: As with smoking, keep all inflammable materials, electrolysis and silver cleaning away from naked flames.

Spillage: In general, all cleaning where finds are immersed in liquids should be carried out within a contained waterproof area, large enough to hold all the liquid should it be spilt from the holding vessel; then any spillages can be returned to service or disposed of safely. Cat litter trays are ideal for this purpose. Keep a supply of rags or kitchen towel handy for mopping up any spillages immediately.

Tongs and tweezers: Use stainless steel or plastic tongs or tweezers for moving objects in and out of chemical solutions. Tongs are available from cookware shops and photographic shops; plastic tweezers from jewellery trade suppliers.

Tools: Use all tools for the purpose intended and follow any safety advice from the manufacturer and supplier.

Ventilation: Some processes and chemicals give off flammable or toxic gases or fumes, so ensure your working area is well ventilated. Open doors or windows and operate extractor fans as available or necessary.

Wash: your hands thoroughly both before and after dealing with finds.

Worktops and cooking utensils: if you need to use cooking utensils keep them separate from those used for food and only use them for finds processing; don't return them to domestic service afterwards. Similarly all kitchen worktops you have used should be scrubbed down thoroughly after use.

Litter tray and plastic tweezers.

Mechanical Cleaning

Manual Methods

The removal of surface deposits by hand is probably the least risky cleaning method you can employ. There are a range of "tools" that can be used and it is safest to start with the most gentle and work up to harsher devices as necessary. For personal safety, eye protection and gloves are advisable and - if you are chipping away at dry corrosion products - a dust mask should also be worn. When you are sitting down using sharp tools it is a good idea to cover your lap with a cushion or folded towel to protect yourself from severe pain and discomfort if you drop the tool, business end downwards, into your lap.

The secret of successful manual cleaning lies in being able to see the object clearly while you are working on it. To achieve this it is essential to use good "hands-free" magnifying apparatus. Professional conservators tend to use binocular microscopes but they are expensive, even second-hand, and many people find them difficult to work with. A good low-cost alternative is binocular magnifying glasses mounted on a headband or clipped onto spectacles. Alternatively, there is a range of desk-mounted or free-standing magnifiers.

A range of "hands free" magnifiers.

Before we start, a word of caution: if you are working on soft metals or fragile surfaces you should avoid brushing or scraping across the surface, even with something soft like a cotton bud, as any grit caught up could leave a nasty scratch in the object. With harsher tools you also risk removing surface detail.

Soaking the object in pure water for a few hours or several days will help soften many deposits so they can be more easily removed. If necessary you can keep putting the object back into soak to soften newly exposed dirt and corrosion surfaces. In the section on chemical cleaning, there are other solutions you can also use.

The most gentle tool is a cotton bud dipped in pure water, which is ideal for cleaning up soft metals like gold where there is usually little corrosion and just dirt sitting in the crevices. Dab or roll the cotton bud against the dirt until it is all absorbed into the cotton bud. You may need to use a few cotton buds depending on how much dirt there is.

Moving up the scale, wooden cocktail sticks or toothpicks can be used quite effectively to remove relatively soft deposits. Again, these are best used vertically working from around the edge of the deposit into its centre. Try and pick at the deposit rather than scrape it.

The only tool that I recommend that you rub across the surface of an object, where necessary, is an ink eraser. Basically you just rub firmly across the surface of the object, which polishes the high points and allows it to be deciphered. This is ideal for bringing out detail in very flat objects like 17th century tokens, jettons and worn Roman coins.

A 17th century token before and after rubbing with an ink eraser.

Now we get to the heavy stuff: metal tools. While wooden picks will bend or break if excessive pressure is applied, metal ones won't. It only needs a force of half a kilogram applied to a fine point to apply several tonnes per square centimetre pressure; so not surprisingly it is quite easy to cause extensive damage to an object.

There are a variety of metal tools that can be used. A scalpel is fairly easy to use and will cope well with all but the hardest deposits. Swann-Morton is a well-established scalpel manufacturer, and handles and blades can be bought from most model and craft shops. The most popular handle is number 3 or 3L (long) and convex blades number 10 or 15 are the most suitable for our purpose. The slightly larger handles number 4, 4L and 5 can also be used and you should use blades 20, 21, 22, 22A, 23 or 24 with these handles.

Dental tools or picks are also very good, particularly for finer work and awkward shapes. I begged a few "cast-off" tools from my dentist and if you go this route just be grateful for what you can get, as you can always grind points or chisel ends on the tools to suit. Dental tools are also available from specialist suppliers listed in the back of the book.

For very fine work and very hard deposits, you will find a sewing or darning needle, mounted in a pin vice or other suitable "handle" invaluable, but remember the sharper the point the more damage can be done if you apply too much pressure or slip. To speed up the process you can use an electric oscillating engraving tool (rotary tools are likely to damage the object's surface) fitted with a carbide point. When using these tools you should not apply any pressure (let the tool do the work) and, if you are using the tool correctly, when corrosion breaks away the tool stays put and does not damage the metal surface. One possible health problem associated with regular use of vibrating power tools is hand-arm vibration syndrome (HAVS). This is an occupational hazard rather than a hobby one, but if you become fanatical about using electric engraving tools it is something to bear in mind.

You will need to keep the working edge of any of the tools sharp, which can be achieved by sharpening on a carborundum stone or replacing the working "tip". For example scalpel blades are particularly prone to blunt quite quickly in use but you can either sharpen the blade or replace it.

The Swann-Morton scalpel has a bayonet fixing for the blade and changing scalpel blades can be a bit tricky until you get used to it. To fit a blade, hold the sharp end in its outer foil wrapper and slide the socket partially onto the bayonet then remove the wrapper and holding the handle push the tip of the blade against a piece of scrap wood so that the blade slides home. To remove the blade grip the top rear of the blade in a pair of pliers and carefully lift the rear of the blade above the bayonet and slide the blade off the handle. When the scalpel isn't being used it is best to either remove the blade or push the tip of the blade into a cork. Used blades should be wrapped in thick card and taped up before disposal.

Whatever tool you are using the method is basically the same. The object is best firmly held and supported in a machine vice, which will also prevent damaged fingers. The jaws should be soft rubber covered (or use chamois leather if the jaws are steel) to protect the object being held and also supported beneath with a strip of wood.

Start no more than a millimetre in from the edge of the corrosion and (electric engravers excepted) apply light vertical pressure (excessive pressure will dent or pit the surface of the metal underneath) and the edge of the corrosion will break off. Move not more than another millimetre in and repeat the process. If you move the tool too far in from the edge of the corrosion it puts an enormous strain on the object, which could shatter. As the corrosion dust builds up it should be periodically removed with a very soft bristle artist's brush or a blower brush used for camera lenses. Do not be tempted to scrape the dust off using the tool that you are breaking the corrosion off with. Obviously, any corrosion left after brushing off will need to be tackled as previously. It is a slow painstaking process but eventually the job will be finished and you should be pleased with the results.

Other tools that can be useful for some manual cleaning are brushes and wire wool. Apart from the plastic bristle varieties already mentioned, brushes are available - in order of harshness - glass fibre, brass and steel. For cleaning iron objects a steel brush is useful to remove surface rust; the object can then be finished off with coarse, medium then fine wire wool. Other than that I rarely use glass fibre or metal brushes for anything except modern finds, such as decimal coins, as they are prone to leave surface scratches which would then need polishing out with jewellers rouge (even though the pencil type can be softened by extending the bristles). As well as scratching, brass brushes also coat the object with a brass film, which can be unsightly on anything other than brass objects. One use I do have for a glass fibre pencil brush, however, is for cleaning the edge of an object to make good contact for electrolysis (to be covered later).

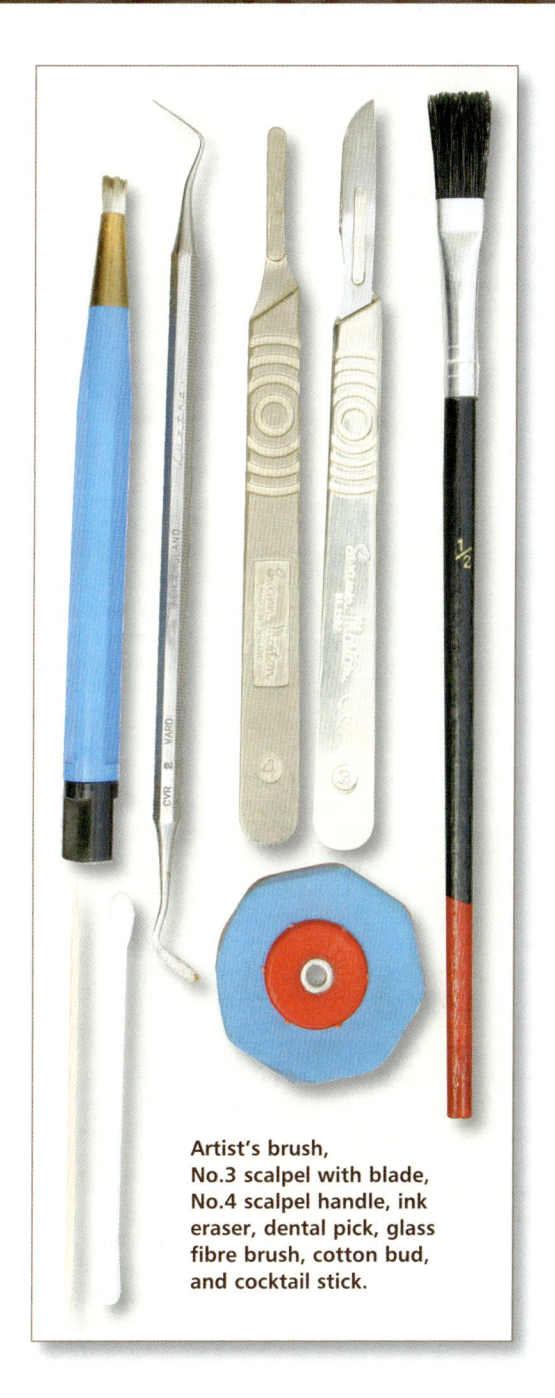

Artist's brush,
No.3 scalpel with blade,
No.4 scalpel handle, ink eraser, dental pick, glass fibre brush, cotton bud, and cocktail stick.

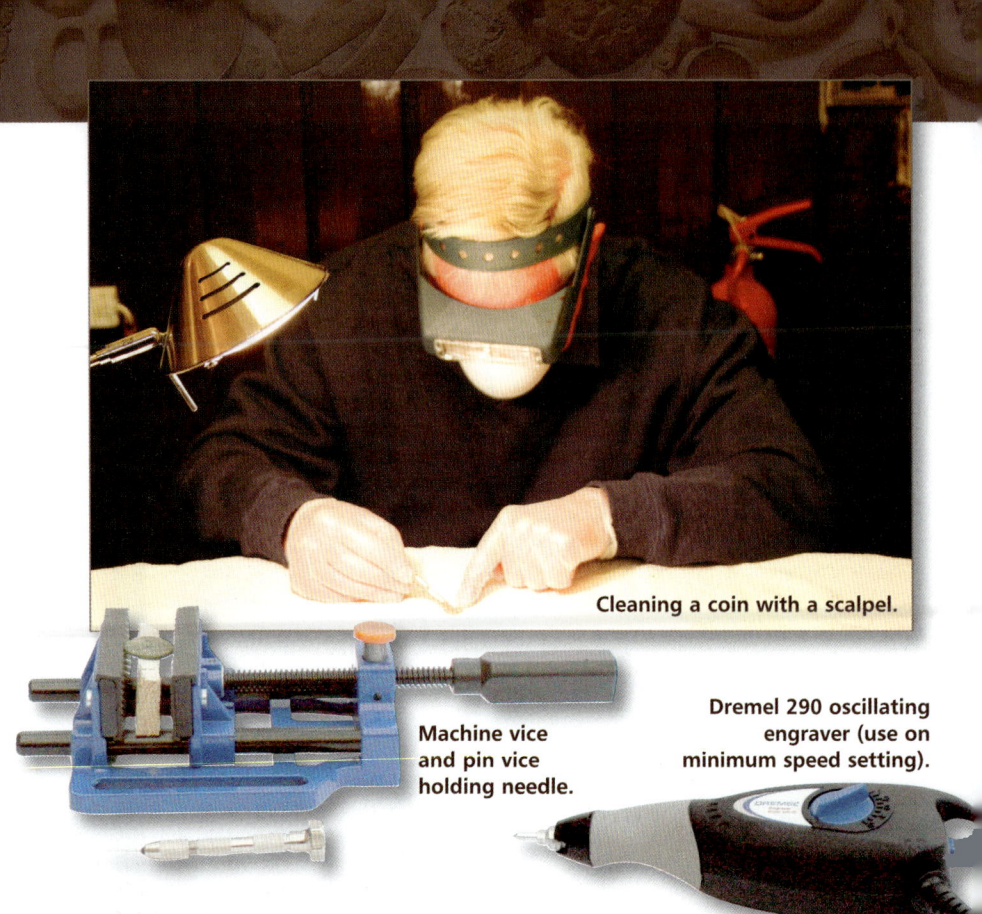

Cleaning a coin with a scalpel.

Machine vice and pin vice holding needle.

Dremel 290 oscillating engraver (use on minimum speed setting).

Cleaning a coin with an oscillating engraver.

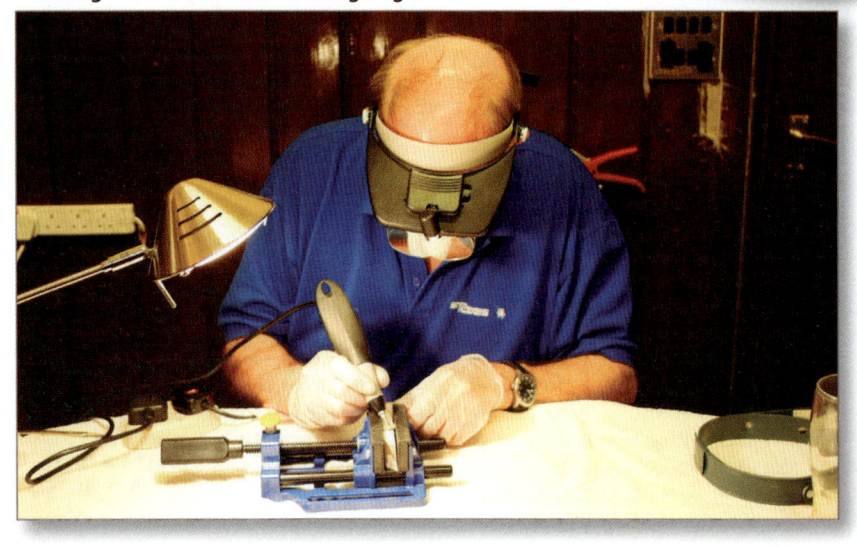

Ultrasonic Cleaners

The ultrasonic cleaner consists of a tank through which ultrasonic waves (usually from 15-400kHz) are passed. The object (or objects, providing they don't overlap one another) to be cleaned are placed in the tank, which is partially filled with warm water at around 50° C to which a drop or two of washing-up liquid can be added to lower the surface tension of the water. The washing-up liquid effectively makes water "wetter", allowing better penetration of the surface detail of the object. The cleaner runs on a timed cycle during which the sound waves cause energy to be released through cavitation or the generation and collapse of millions of microscopic bubbles. These break up dirt and contaminants from the object, usually in a few minutes. Ultrasonic cleaners are readily available from some metal detector dealers, electronic retailers, the jewellery trade, hobby suppliers and even some supermarkets.

Providing they are used with care, these cleaners are probably the most useful mechanical cleaner available. They have a double use in that they can remove dirt and corrosion in their own right without the use of harsh chemicals, and can also be used to thoroughly wash a find after it has been chemically treated. Bear in mind, however, that there is a tendency for bright spots to appear on chemically treated objects where they touch the tank or the basket insert. Fragile objects, particularly anything that is already cracked, should not be subjected to ultrasonic cleaning; neither should enamelled or delicately plated objects, nor soft metals like aluminium and lead, which may become pitted during the process. Beware also of losing loose stones from jewellery.

Although most, if not all, ultrasonic cleaner suppliers offer an enhanced chemical cleaning solution for use with their machines, I would only use this very sparingly, if at all, and follow it with a plain wash cycle to remove all traces of chemicals. Bear in mind also that the ultrasonic action exaggerates the damaging effects of chemicals by allowing deeper penetration into the object; using your own recipes directly in the tank, particularly acids or bleach, risks ruining not only your find but the cleaner as well. There is, however a way that you can use some chemicals in the cleaner without risking damaging the cleaner by what is known as the "indirect method". You must never use solvents like alcohol or acetone in an ultrasonic cleaner either by the direct or indirect method because the process generates heat and rapid evaporation, and the vapours may ignite with dire consequences.

Using the indirect method you can submerge the object in the chemical solution in a small container, which you place directly into the tank, then fill the tank up carefully to its usual operating level with water and operate the cleaner as normal. Glass containers are recommended but plastic containers with the lid fitted work fine. They should float in the tank water and the lid will prevent any exchange of fluid between the container and tank. Using chemicals by the indirect method can still be as damaging to finds as by the direct method; however, in some circumstances such as patination pre-treatment, discussed later, the cleaning is superior to alternative methods.

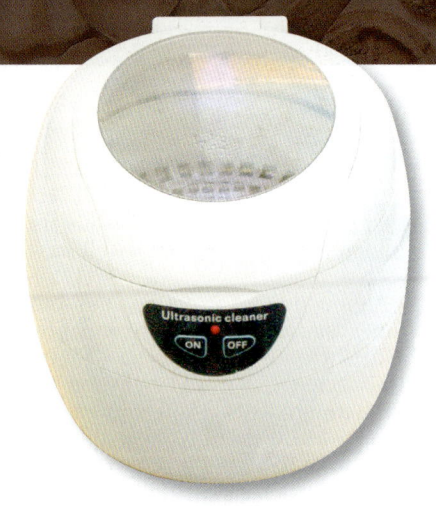

Ultrasonic cleaner.

Barrelling Machines

Barrelling machines, available from many metal detector retailers, consist of an electrically driven internally finned plastic drum into which you seal up to 10 or so objects to be cleaned, with steel shapes, soap and water. Typically, the cleaning cycle is around four hours. I have used one of these machines, the same one, for more than 30 years and although I have gone through a number of drive belts and drum caps that machine is still going strong.

The one danger with these machines is that the plastic drum end caps are a tight push fit onto the drum; sometimes they leak water and every so often a cap will split in use and discharge half a drum of water or so over the motor housing. So far my machine has withstood dousing several times but be prepared. Run the machine in a plastic tray large enough so that the vents to the electric motor will remain well out of the liquid if the entire drum empties itself in use or, if the tray is too small, stand the machine on a plinth of wood, tiles or similar. You can test this by filling the drum with water then pouring it into the tray and making sure the liquid level doesn't come above the vents. In practice you'll seldom fill the drum over half anyway.

A couple of tips for users of these machines: the first is that the drum can roll off the machine in the direction of rotation so stand the machine to leave ample space in the tray to catch the drum if it rolls off. The second tip is that if you have trouble getting the drum to start rotating, lift the tray slightly by wedging a thin piece of wood under it so that the drum is leaning harder against the drive roller.

Barrelling is very harsh and, depending on the length of treatment, polishes metal to a satin or bright finish, removing surface metal in the process - and also any plating, inlay or enamel. Older finds may come out pitted as the process scours out deeply embedded corrosion, so this treatment is best used for the bulk treatment of robust modern finds such as modern coinage and brass badges. Special burnishing soap is sold by barrelling machine suppliers and this is designed to be used at the rate of around one tablespoon per charge, to give the best polish effect for army badges and the like. A tablespoon of pure soap flakes or a squirt of washing up liquid can be used instead if a high lustre isn't necessary. Barrelling different alloys together will result in some strange colour finishes as the objects tend to plate each other. So brass, copper, cupro-nickel and silver (if you must) should all be treated in separate batches. With bimetallic objects like our modern £2 coin you can choose to put them in either a brass or a cupro-nickel batch, treat them one at a time or use a different cleaning method. The harshness of the treatment can be controlled firstly by the volume of water in the drum; the higher the volume, the more gentle the treatment. Secondly, cleaning can be controlled by the length of treatment time.

Unfortunately, you cannot see what is going on inside the drum but you can stop the treatment at, say, hourly intervals, pour the contents through a strong sieve into a jug and check the progress. Remove and wash any completed objects, add others if desired and put everything back in the drum for another session. Like most things, with practice you will have a good idea at the outset how long cleaning will take and even if you get it wrong you're not likely to get arrested for defacing the queen's coinage.

On the final turn-out wash the shapes thoroughly and spread them out in a shallow container, dab with kitchen towel and leave them in a warm place to dry or else they will rust. Don't be too concerned if the shapes go rusty, they'll clean up the next time you use them.

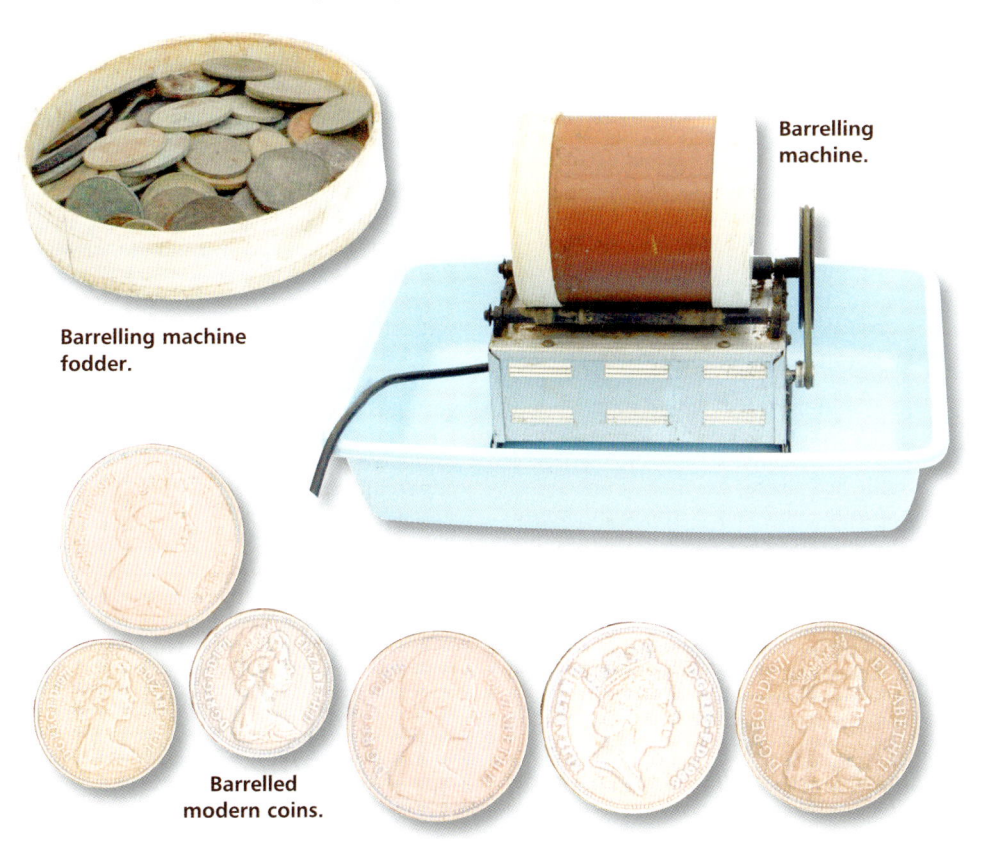

Barrelling machine.

Barrelling machine fodder.

Barrelled modern coins.

39

Electrolysis

Electrolysis involves the passing of a low voltage direct electric current (DC) through the object to be cleaned and a dilute chemical solution called an electrolyte, in which the object is suspended. The object to be cleaned forms the negative electrode or cathode, while the other side of the circuit, the positive electrode or anode is scrap stainless steel; the corrosion removed is passed into solution as well as being re-deposited on the anode. Electrolysis works by releasing hydrogen gas from the water at the cathode, which attacks and gradually eliminates the corrosion.

If you thought barrelling was harsh, electrolysis is "Oh my God be careful!" and definitely a last resort - the last drink in the last chance saloon! Electrolysis can strip to bare metal in minutes, which may be okay for silver but not so good for copper-alloys. Plating, inlays and enamels will definitely be lost. The act of passing electricity through metals physically alters their structure and I have seen lumps of corrosion on silver objects reduced to solid silver so you can end up with a silver object covered in silver warts and the process is irreversible. Some ancient bronze objects contain quantities of lead, which is distributed in globules and selectively removed by electrolysis leaving ugly pits. Not only that, but the removed lead goes into solution and can plate the bronze. You have been warned! However, if you have a heavily encrusted object, no other way of cleaning it, and you are prepared to risk total loss, electrolysis may just produce wonderful results. It is also quite suitable for lead and lead alloys where their softness tends to preclude mechanical cleaning.

There are also three personal hazards to be aware of in the use of electrolysis, the main being the use of electricity with water. The electrolysis "tank" should be stood within a suitable plastic tray, while the power source should remain outside the tray or in its own smaller tray within the main tray providing it is of sufficient depth to protect the power source from total spillage of the tank.

The second hazard is that hydrogen gas is given off which is not only inflammable but readily forms explosive mixtures with air, which apparently can happen inside the body - so good ventilation, no smoking, no naked flames etc. Finally, because of the escape of gas the electrolyte can splash and it may become more harmful as the cleaning proceeds.

Some metal detector dealers sell "switch on and go" electrolysis kits, which undoubtedly work and are usually supplied with everything you need to get started (except perhaps water and a clothes peg). You can, however, build your own kit fairly easily. The main part is a transformer, usually called an adaptor, with an output of up to 12 volts DC. You will also need a plastic container of around a litre capacity, a couple of crocodile clips (preferably a red one and a black one), a clothes peg and a piece of scrap stainless steel (ie an item of cutlery such as an old spoon). If you haven't found any stainless steel and can't find any redundant in the kitchen, try a charity shop.

It is preferable to have a transformer or adaptor with a means of varying the voltage, which gives much more control of the process. Maplin Electronics supply a range of variable voltage AC (mains) adaptors, which have switch selectable outputs of 3, 4.5, 6, 7.5, 9 and 12 volts DC. There are a number of current ratings and all will work but aim for 1000mA-1500mA (1Amp-1.5Amps), which will be fairly robust and less likely to trip out on thermal overload during prolonged use. Although it is overkill for our purpose, you could also use a car battery charger with dual voltage, 6 and 12 volt DC output.

If you have a spare adaptor in the 4.5v-12v range you can always start with that but don't use one you need for anything else as you will have to cut the output plug, or power tip, off as you will have to do also with the Maplin adaptor. Most adaptors have two wires (their sleeves are lightly welded together) on the output side, one all black, which should be the negative, the other black and white, which should be the positive.

Get your adaptor and remove the power tip by cutting through the output wiring with pliers, as close to the power tip as possible. Pull the two wires apart for about 10cm (4 inches) and strip off the end 1cm (half inch) of insulation or sleeve on each wire. Twist each of the bare wire ends to consolidate the strands. Fill your plastic container with water and place the two bare wire ends in the water a few inches apart making sure they don't touch. Plug in your adaptor, switch on and look carefully at the wires in the water, one of them should be fizzing, write down the colour or mark that wire with a piece of tape to identify it. That should be the black wire but nevertheless fix the black crocodile clip to it and fix the red crocodile clip to the other wire.

Electrolysis cleaners can work extraordinarily well, but the one area where they leave a lot to be desired is the method for attaching the object to be cleaned. The usual method is to hold the object in a crocodile clip, which has to bite through the corrosion to make an electrical connection often scarring the object in the process. Also the crocodile clips are usually plated steel which quickly corrode; brass would be better but they are very uncommon nowadays. Another method is to make a hanger from stiff bare copper wire, which is slightly better but can still scratch the object. My solution is to use 28mm copper pipe clips (spacing), which can be bent to grip the object, particularly a coin, safely on its edge after first brushing the contact area with a glass fibre brush to ensure a good connection. Avoid using the brush on other types of object though.

To make the holder using pipe clips you will need to take two of the smaller spacers and join one each side of a larger clip using brass nuts and bolts, then remodel the pliable spacers so that they hook over each side of the plastic container. The central clip can be adjusted to hold different sized objects. Eventually the parts used in the solution will disintegrate, so hold on to the other clips, spacers, nuts and bolts that inevitably come in small packs, so you can repair and remake holders as required.

The current popular electrolyte is citric acid and salt solution. I think it is a good idea to avoid salt but if you want to use citric acid make up a 1% solution (10 grams in a litre of pure water) and you will have to add half a teaspoon of salt to get the current to flow. I prefer to use a 5% solution (50 grams in a litre of pure water) of either sodium carbonate (washing soda), sodium bicarbonate (baking soda) or better still for copper-alloys, a 50/50 mixture of the two which is equivalent to sodium sesquicarbonate. There is a high risk of unwanted

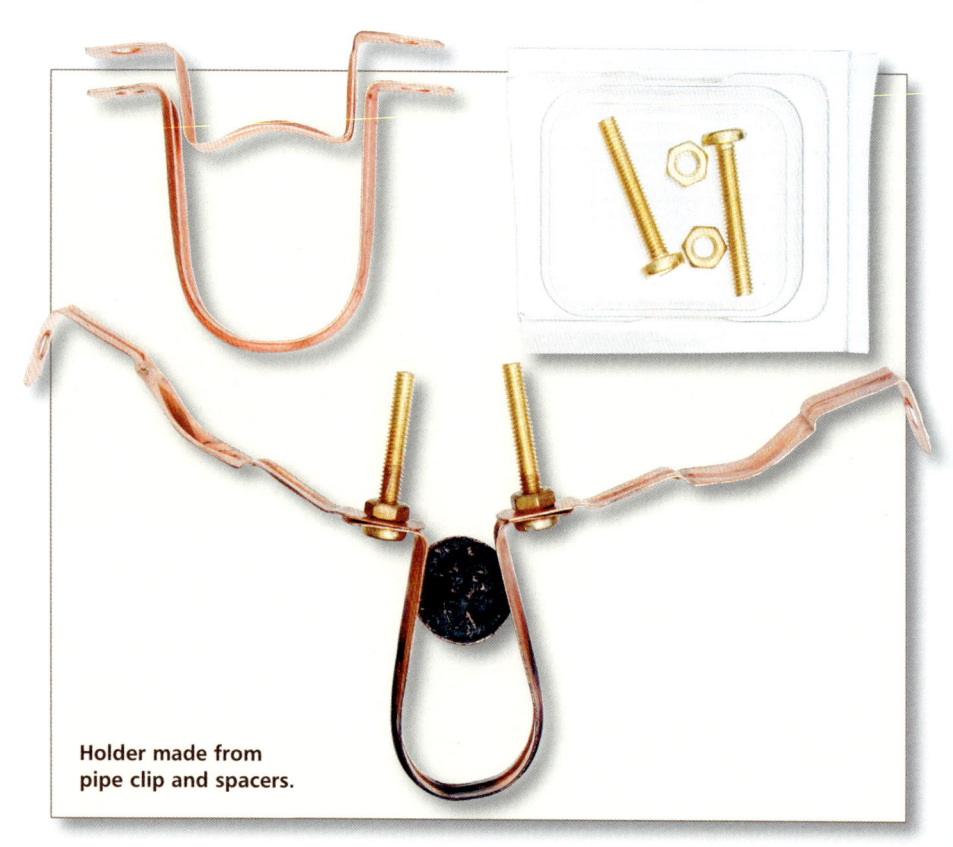

Holder made from pipe clip and spacers.

plating occurring if different metals are cleaned in the same solution so two separate tanks, one for silver cleaning and a second for base metals would be ideal. Alternatively, a good wash-up would be necessary when changing from one metal to another. Electrolyte can be stored in labelled plastic bottles for reuse until it gets very dirty, when a fresh batch should be made up. If you have two tanks made from plastic containers with lids, you can remove the electrodes and store the electrolyte in the tank with the lid on.

Cleaning is achieved by mounting the object in the cathode or negative clamp (black) and ensuring it is completely submerged in the electrolyte. Ensure the transformer is *not* turned on and clip the stainless steel anode to the inside of the plastic tank with a clothes peg so that it is touching the bottom of the tank a few inches away from but directly opposite the object and partly submerged in the electrolyte. Connect the transformer or adaptor to a suitable 13-amp mains socket and turn it on at low voltage say 4.5 volts, if you have that option. Gradually increase the voltage as necessary until you see a steady stream of small bubbles coming from the object. The newer Maplin adaptors have to be unplugged from wall sockets to change the voltage so carefully remove the cathode complete with object out of the solution and return once the voltage is changed and the power is back on.

If there are no bubbles, assuming the hardware is wired up and working correctly, carefully move the cathode, nearer to the stainless steel anode. If bubbling becomes very vigorous, back off the voltage or move the cathode further from the anode.

The amount of electrolysis required varies very much from object to object but err on the side of caution and start with just one minute. After a minute, carefully remove the object (avoid touching the anode with the object as this could damage the transformer or adaptor) then turn off the power. If you turn off the power first, there is a great risk of the object becoming plated. Wipe the object gently with a wet paper towel, tissue or toothbrush, then rinse in clean water. Carefully examine the object to assess the degree of cleaning achieved and if further electrolysis is required, resume cleaning for another minute followed by a wet wipe and further checking. If little or no cleaning has occurred, double-up on the time between checks and keep doubling until you get results (eg 2 minutes, 5 minutes, 10 minutes, 20 minutes etc.); some objects take several hours. Once the object has been cleaned enough, put it to soak and rest in pure water for 24 hours. Always remove and clean the anode before commencing cleaning the next object, even if it is the same metal and if the electrolyte level has dropped through evaporation, top-up with pure water.

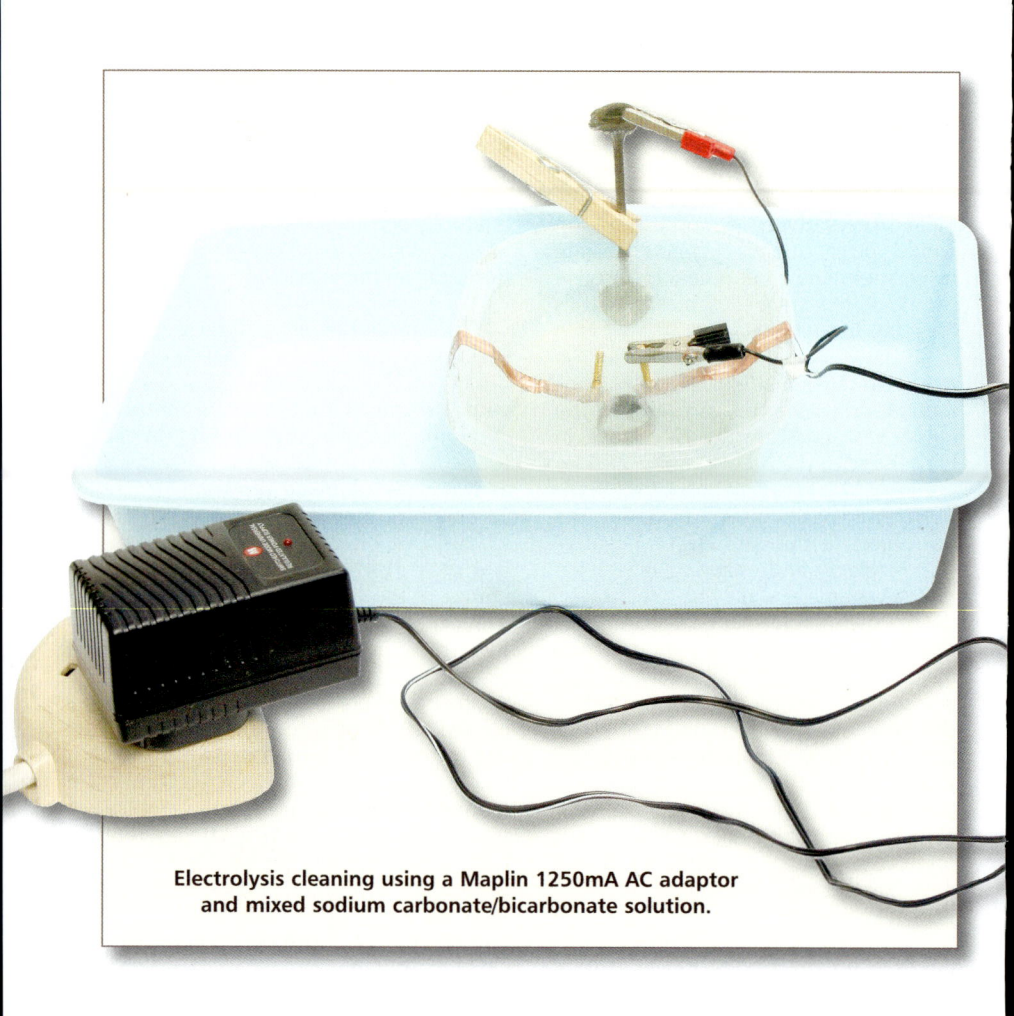

Electrolysis cleaning using a Maplin 1250mA AC adaptor and mixed sodium carbonate/bicarbonate solution.

Chemical Cleaning & Conservation

Most of the chemicals we'll be using are domestic, so in themselves they are not too obnoxious; however, we will often be using them in ways they weren't really intended to be used in the home and that could give rise to problems. I will point out the known dangers, but be aware that the corrosive products - and hence the chemistry - will undoubtedly differ from object to object and there might be nasty surprises. Only use these treatments if you are confident in doing so and whatever you do, please take precautions. At least wear waterproof gloves and eye protection and handle chemicals carefully at arm's length, so that any spitting or splashing is away from your face.

As the chemistry of every object will differ, there is not going to be one right way and one wrong way to clean a particular object. It will be very much a case of trial, error, experience and personal preference. Under-cleaning is preferable to over-cleaning. Slow and steady wins the race and shortcuts lead to long delays. Bear in mind that there is nothing at all wrong with doing a bit of chemical cleaning, which will loosen and soften encrustation then switching to mechanical cleaning or even electrolysis then back to chemical cleaning and so on until the job is done. All we want is good results, which should get even better with practice.

If you have localised areas of corrosion it is better to dab the chemical onto the area with a cotton bud so that the chemical only works where it is needed. However, more often than not, corrosion covers the whole object and soaking is necessary if you are going to use chemical treatments. So to get started we need a few small plastic containers with lids to minimise evaporation so the solution won't increase in strength or dry out over time; the smallest of the food container range (150-200ml) will be about right. Label the containers with the solution name in permanent marker on the side and on the lid so you know exactly what is where and there won't then be any mishaps. I'm sure you will realise that you only need to cover the object completely with the solution, it is not necessary to fill the container.

All references to "pure water" means the best quality water you can obtain, ideally it should be distilled water but as that is now quite difficult to get hold of, de-ionised water is quite acceptable (but see washing in the "Identification and Assessment" chapter).

Chemicals

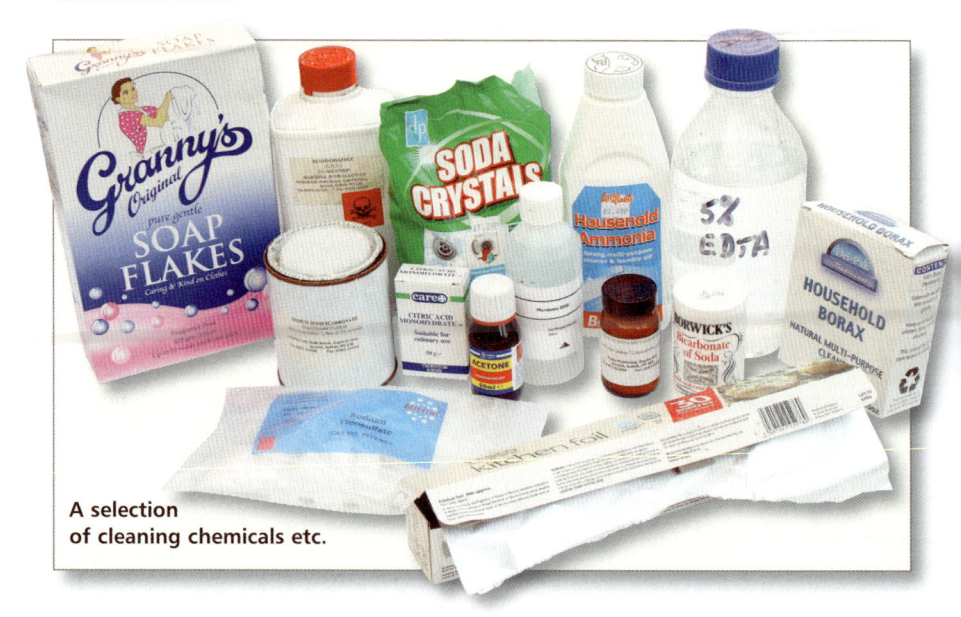

A selection of cleaning chemicals etc.

Making Solutions

Nearly all the chemicals that are used for cleaning are supplied in solid form and need to be dissolved in a liquid (usually pure water) before they can be used. The technique is fairly simple once you've tried it a couple of times and all you need is an accurate weighing device (measuring in grams), and a means of measuring volume, preferably in millilitres (ml) but centilitres (10ml), or even decilitres (100ml) will suffice. You may come across the volumetric measurement: cubic centimetre (cc) which is exactly the same as a millilitre. If you are buying chemicals from a metal detector dealer you will usually be supplied with a quality plastic storage bottle and instructions. Some of the chemicals we will be using are domestic and come as they are. Washed-out plastic milk containers, while not being the strongest, are readily available in useful one pint or half litre (500ml) and two pint or one litre (1000ml). If you want smaller containers then soft drinks bottles are quite usable in 250ml and 330ml. It is vital, for your own sake and everyone around you, that you clearly re-label any domestic containers you use with the precise contents in permanent marker.

The main solutions we will be making up are solids dissolved in liquid at a weight to volume ratio (w/v). The concentration is given in percent, which means the number of grams dissolved in 100 millilitres of liquid. (Not the number of grams dissolved in a litre, which is 1000 millilitres). For example, a 5% solution is 5 grams in 100ml; 10 grams in 200ml; 12.5 grams in 250ml; 25 grams in 500ml and 50 grams in a litre. I'm sure you can pro-rata any other percentages and volumes from that. Using milk containers, which have wide necks, it is quite easy to pour the solid into the container via a rolled up sheet of paper made into a funnel and then to add liquid up to the half litre or litre mark as appropriate. You then put the top on and shake until the solid is dissolved. I wouldn't worry if some of the solid doesn't dissolve as it will probably do so, eventually, of its own accord. Warming water beforehand will help the solid dissolve faster but it is highly dangerous to warm solvents like alcohol.

A few solutions are liquid diluted with another liquid at a volume to volume ratio (v/v). This is similar to the above except the percentage is a measure of the number of millilitres in 100 millilitres. For example a 5% solution is 5 millilitres in 100ml; 10 millilitres in 200ml; 12.5 millilitres in 250ml; 25 millilitres in 500ml, and 50 millilitres in a litre.

If you want to change the concentration of an existing solution you can add a measured amount of the appropriate solid to make it stronger (eg to make a litre of 5% solution into a litre of 10% solution, add 50 grams of the appropriate solid and dissolve. To reduce the concentration of an existing solution just add a measured amount of water or appropriate solvent (eg to reduce 500ml of 10% solution to 5%, add 500ml of water or appropriate solvent which will make a litre of solution at 5% concentration).

Before we start the important thing to remember about chemical cleaning is that over time the solution and the object will reach equilibrium where either the active ingredient is neutralised or all used up or the solution becomes saturated with contaminants and can't absorb any more. Often there will be a physical change where the solution becomes dirty or changes colour and sometimes there can be harmful by-products; so it is necessary to regularly discard the used solution and replace with fresh. As a rule of thumb if there is no noticeable change to the object being cleaned or the solution over a period of 24 hours, then renew the solution; if this produces no change over the next 24 hours, then change the treatment.

1. Pure water - all metals except iron. If we have to clean, the mildest treatment we can give any non-ferrous metal object is to soak it in pure water. Soak it for about 24 hours and if the water is dirty it is doing its job so change the water and repeat the process. It is fine to brush the object gently with a soft brush or for fragile objects roll a cotton bud over between soaks, the more dirt and debris we can take off, the better.

2. Soap solution - all metals except iron. Most washing up liquids and powders contain additives, which may be harmful. Teepol make a neutral laboratory grade liquid detergent if you can get hold of it (bear in mind Teepol make formulations for the domestic market which will be no different for our purposes than other brands). The best you can probably do is to buy pure soap flakes from a supermarket etc, and make up a 0.5% solution (5 grams in a litre of pure water). It is quite difficult to dissolve the soap flakes so it is best to heat up the water in a kettle (don't get it too hot or your plastic container will melt, let the water cool a little before you use it, if necessary). If you use Teepol the recommended concentration will be 5ml in a litre of pure water). Soak your object for 24 hours and check and brush it etc. All the while dirt is coming off, keep soaking. This treatment may be all that is required for lightly soiled objects, but once you have finished the treatment you will need to remove the soap residue; to do that you go back and repeat the first stage, pure water, until all evidence of soap, bubbles etc. has been removed.

3. Acid treatment - all metals. This is just one route of treatment, which will suit the olive oil and lemon juice brigades. As you have probably guessed, I am not going to recommend either of those natural, or fairly natural, substances. Olive oil is very mildly acidic at 0.3% to 3%, depending on factors such as where the olives are grown. It is also a variable mixture of ingredients, so you won't know what is in the mixture and cleaning results will vary from one bottle to the next. Worse than that, oil is very difficult to near impossible to remove from objects and can trap moisture with the effect that corrosion continues or worsens. The main active ingredient of lemon juice is citric acid, which varies between 4.5% and about 10%, and again contains a variable mixture of substances; so your cleaning results will vary from lemon to lemon. Bottled lemon juice is probably more consistent but on the other hand contains additives, which may be harmful to finds.

What I am going to propose is that you use citric acid crystals, which are available from some metal detector dealers and, being used in home wine and beer making, are readily available from high street chemists etc. As a substitute for olive oil use a 1% citric acid solution (10 grams in a litre of pure water), which will soften encrustation for mechanical removal as well as gently cleaning objects in their own right. You can leave the object in soak for a few days up to a few weeks. You will need to mechanically remove any lumps of corrosion and to turn the object over every day or so to even out the cleaning on both sides. If the solution stops working before all the corrosion has been removed, it would be prudent to replace the solution, as the acid will have become exhausted.

As a substitute for lemon juice use a 5% citric acid solution (50 grams in a litre of pure water) and this works well on all metals (particularly copper-alloys and silver alloys showing green corrosion), including iron, as citric acid is used commercially for rust removal. These citric acid solutions will strip down to bare metal eventually and may attack the metal itself so their best use is as a corrosion softener to aid mechanical cleaning. If cleaning is happening too fast, just dilute the solution down until you are happy with the results. (See: After Cleaning Treatment).

4. Sodium hexametaphosphate (SHMP) - mainly copper-alloys. A non-corrosive chemical for rapidly removing dirt and corrosion deposits from copper-alloys, while, with care, keeping the patina intact. Use a 10% solution (100 grams in a litre of pure water), soak for 10 minutes and then brush or swab off in pure water. Repeat as necessary but beware SHMP will eventually strip the object down to bare metal. (See: After Cleaning Treatment).

5. Jeweller's stock - mainly silver and precious metals. I'm not a great fan of potions but this is a traditional jewellery cleaner made up from fairly readily obtainable household cleaning chemicals that apart from ammonia fumes (irritant, so make and use in a well-ventilated area), aren't too obnoxious. All the chemicals are available at supermarkets, pound stores, hardware stores, chemists, etc. For a litre of solution you will need:-

Household borax - 13 grams
Washing soda - 6 grams
Pure soap flakes - 5 grams
Household ammonia (9.5%) - 85 millilitres
Pure water - 915 millilitres

This is probably a similar formula to "Silver Dip" and will remove tarnish and corrosion from silver and gold without appearing to attack the metal; but use sparingly and swab or soak for 10 minutes at a time. It could also be used on copper-alloys but it strips down to bare metal very fast. (See: After Cleaning Treatment).

6. Sodium bicarbonate and aluminium foil - silver. The black tarnish often found on silver is silver sulphide; this can be removed by setting up an electrochemical reaction with aluminium foil and an alkaline solution. Sodium bicarbonate is called by other names such as bicarbonate of soda, baking soda (not baking powder which is a mixture of sodium bicarbonate and tartaric acid) or bicarb. Other alkalis such as sodium carbonate (washing soda) or saliva can be used but will not work as well as sodium bicarbonate and what's more I dread to think what you might have had in your mouth.

The method works wonderfully well for coins as it tends to brighten the high spots and leave the lower parts darker; therefore you achieve a contrast allowing features and legends to be easily identified. Cut a piece of baking foil large enough to wrap up the object, lay the object on the foil, wet the object with 5% sodium bicarbonate solution (50 grams in a litre of pure water) and wrap the foil around the object smoothing the foil with your fingers. Heat is generated in the reaction and hydrogen sulphide gas is given off that - apart from smelling of bad eggs - is a toxic and inflammable gas; good ventilation is needed but naked flames and lighted cigarettes definitely aren't! Repeat the process as many times as necessary to achieve the desired result. If necessary you can screw the aluminium into a loose ball and gently rub the blackened areas; however, there is a risk of scratching the object and it might be better to use electrolysis for any object not responding to the foil wrapping treatment. (See: After Cleaning Treatment). The object can be gently polished with a silver polishing cloth afterwards if desired.

7. Sodium thiosulphate - silver mainly but can be used in place of SSC on copper-alloys. The principal use for sodium thiosulphate is in traditional photographic development as a fixative, so it is available from photographic suppliers and often called "hypo". As it is used in photography

to remove silver halides, it can be used effectively to remove silver chloride (a halide) or horn silver, which shows as a purple-grey to dark grey crust on silver objects. Swab or soak the object in a 5% sodium thiosulphate solution (50 grams in a litre of pure water) for 10 minutes then check and gently brush the object. Repeat as necessary. (See: After Cleaning Treatment). Silver objects can be gently polished with a silver polishing cloth afterwards if desired.

8. Ethylene diamine tetra-acetic acid (EDTA) - mainly lead, lead alloys and iron. EDTA is excellent at dissolving metal oxides, particularly (white) lead oxide and iron oxide, better known as rust. It is available from some metal detector dealers and should be made up into a 5% solution (50 grams in a litre of pure water). Simply swab or soak the object until the deposits are dissolved. (See: After Cleaning Treatment).

9. Alcohol/Acetone - all metals. These solvents are used as supplied for degreasing, cleaning and drying of any metals and to dissolve some substances that are near to insoluble in water. All are highly inflammable and volatile; the fumes can be harmful if inhaled so use in a well-ventilated area, free from naked flames, and keep containers tightly covered. Wear gloves when using solvents as oils in the skin can transfer back onto the object and the removal of oils from the hands may cause problems such as cracked skin. To use these solvents either brush them over the object thoroughly or soak for 20 minutes.

These solvents can be a problem to get hold of. Mineralised Methylated Spirits (MMS) or Meths is the purple (shades vary) fluid readily available from hardware shops etc. However, it contains pyridine, which will leave harmful deposits on metal objects, so only use MMS if you have a purer alcohol or acetone you can use for a final rinse. Industrial Methylated Spirits (IMS), now called Industrial Denatured Alcohol (IDA) does not contain pyridine and is widely used by conservators; however, unless you are willing to pay about £20 per litre excise duty, you need to obtain a free licence from Customs and Excise, which will allow you to use up to 20 litres per year in your hobby, under section 17.8 of *Production, distribution and use of denatured alcohol HMRC Notice 473* (July 2005).

Other alcohols you can use are Industrial Alcohol or rubbing alcohol, which is iso-propanol or iso-propyl alcohol (IPA) and methyl alcohol or methanol, which are free from customs restrictions. Acetone is not an alcohol but is also quite acceptable and is more widely available than IPA and methanol as it is commonly used for nail varnish remover; however, there is a trend to make it more user attractive by adding colour and perfume which we want to avoid for our purposes.

The next problem is that Royal Mail won't transport solvents; so you either need to collect from the supplier or find one that uses a suitable carrier. IPA and acetone are both used as solvents in glass fibre construction projects so are available from suppliers in this area such as yacht chandlers and some car accessory suppliers. Acetone is available at high street chemists.

After Cleaning Treatment

With the exception of the solvents just mentioned (other than MMS), it is essential that all remains of chemicals used are removed otherwise corrosion may continue or even get worse! If the object is robust and not plated, inlaid or enamelled and you have an ultrasonic cleaner, then you can give it a normal cycle in pure water in the cleaner but bear in mind that you may get bright spots on the object where it touches the tank. Otherwise you will need to soak it in a soap solution (see page 47) then soak it in pure water (see page 47). Iron should not be put in water or soap solution, otherwise it will rust; and neither should any object that has been dried using solvents. Blot iron dry with white kitchen towel then soak for 20 minutes in alcohol (except MMS) or acetone to remove any remaining water and chemical.

Specialist Treatments

A Simple Test for Chlorides

The following treatments involve the removal of chlorides from copper-alloy and iron objects to prevent their total destruction. The success of the treatments is somewhat hit and miss owing generally to not being able to determine whether all the chlorides have been removed or not. Traditional tests for chlorides involve strong acids and specialist chemicals; however, there is a simple, although not foolproof, test that can be used at any time during the treatment to assess whether chlorides are present in the wash water or not. Once the wash water is clear of chlorides, the object will have been successfully treated but don't forget to check a sample of the water being used to make up the treatment solutions as that may itself test positive for chlorides depending on the quality being used.

Take about 30cm (12 inches) length of copper wire, and strip the end 8cm (3 inches) of insulation off. Twist the strands of bare wire together and fold these back on themselves. Twist together again so you have 4cm (1.5 inches) of bare wire at the end of double thickness. Heat the bare wire up in a blue flame from a gas hob, gas cigarette lighter or spirit lamp, etc, until the flame burns without any green colour. Dip the bare wire in the solution and hold it in the blue flame; if there are chlorides present the flame, or part of it, will turn bright green. Burn the colour off ready for the next test and avoid handling the bare wire with your fingers as the skin excretes chlorides.

Chloride test using a flame.

Treatment of Bronze Disease in Copper-Alloys

Bronze disease is that green to blue or brown powdery substance that looks something like a fungus on old copper-alloy objects. It starts with the formation of copper (cuprous) chloride by a reaction between copper and chlorine from the ground, water or air in the presence of oxygen and moisture. In the burial environment other corrosion products like copper oxide tend to protect the object, but when we excavate or clean the object the disturbance will often trigger a reaction between the cuprous chloride and moisture in the air that will form hydrochloric acid. The acid then dissolves and eats into the copper forming more cuprous chloride, which in turn forms more hydrochloric acid in a chain reaction that can only end with the total destruction of the object, unless we do something to stop it.

If you keep the object in your Dry Box maintained below 35% RH, that will effectively eliminate moisture and stop the reaction so the bronze disease won't get any worse. However, if you want to clean the object and conserve it for display, treatment is available providing you are patient; but you are unlikely to be able to repair any damage already done.

1. Remove as much of the deposit as you can by brushing with a firm toothbrush and use a cocktail stick to pick out any remaining spots. You could also clean it ultrasonically.

2. Soak the object in pure water (distilled or de-ionised) for 10-14 days. This will leach out the acid and halt the process.

3. Degrease the object in alcohol or acetone. Brush the object with the solvent then soak in the solvent for 20 minutes.

4. Soak the object in a 5% solution of sodium sesquicarbonate (SSC), available from some metal detector dealers, for 14 days; brush the object then change the solution for fresh and soak for a further 14 days. A similar solution to sodium sesquicarbonate can be made by mixing sodium carbonate with sodium bicarbonate in equal proportions (dissolve 25 grams of each in a litre of pure water for a 5% solution). These solutions at these concentrations will remove any patinas on objects. If you need to try and save a patina, dilute the solution down to 1% or 2% but you will need to repeat the 14 days soaking period five times to combat the bronze disease.

5. Soak the object in pure water for 7 days.

6. Soak the object for 7 days in a 3% solution of Benzotriazole (BTA) (30 grams in a litre of alcohol or acetone). BTA is available from some metal detector dealers; however, it is said to be a suspected carcinogen, meaning it could cause cancer. I have searched diligently and have not been able to find BTA on any list of carcinogens or suspected carcinogens and a learned source on chemical safety data only says: harmful if swallowed or inhaled. Skin, eye and respiratory irritant; use safety glasses, adequate ventilation, gloves (to which I would add: dust mask). After soaking, remove the object and brush off any loose precipitated BTA. If you have any qualms about using BTA, then don't! Just miss this stage out but soak the object in alcohol or acetone for 20 minutes instead to remove any remaining moisture.

7. Let the object sit in air for 10 days and examine it closely for any signs of bronze disease remaining or returning. If there is any sign whatsoever restart the process from the beginning.

8. Objects apparently cured of bronze disease can be stored in a Dry Box, stored or displayed without further treatment or finished off with a protective coating as discussed in Finishing Treatment. All copper-alloy objects should be periodically checked for signs of bronze disease as a matter of course.

Treatment of Sweating Iron

Iron, which shows tiny drops of rusty water on the surface, is suffering a similar affliction to bronze disease; a chemically similar reaction with iron chlorides and hydrochloric acid is underway, which will rapidly result in total disintegration. The treatment is several washes in an alkaline solution, which can be carried out cold or hot depending on how long you've got (or perhaps how much patience you have).

Traditionally caustic soda (sodium hydroxide) would be used but this is a very corrosive substance, particularly if it gets on flesh, so I would suggest you use 5% (50 grams in a litre of pure water) washing soda (sodium carbonate) solution as a much safer alternative; it is also widely available. The methods are:-

1. Soak the object in sodium carbonate solution for 10 weeks, replacing the solution with fresh at weekly intervals. Or boil the object for 10 hours in sodium carbonate solution, replacing the solution with fresh every hour. Don't use an aluminium pan for this as sodium carbonate attacks aluminium.

2. Soak the object for one week in pure water to remove the sodium carbonate. Or boil the object for 3 hours in pure water, replacing the water with fresh every hour.

3. Wire brush the object to remove fresh corrosion and rinse in pure water.

4. Soak in 25% alcohol/75% water mix for 24 hours.

5. Soak in 50% alcohol/50% water mix for 24 hours.

6. Soak in 75% alcohol/25% water mix for 24 hours.

7. Soak in 100% acetone for 24 hours.

8. Sit the object in air for at least seven days. If there is any sign of sweating, restart the treatment.

9. Mechanically clean the surface with wire brush, picks etc, and swab with 100% alcohol to clean up the dust.

10. Store in a Dry Box or finish with

microcrystalline wax and clear lacquer. (See Finishing Treatments). All iron objects should be periodically checked for signs of sweating as a matter of course.

Finishing Treatments

It is assumed that all necessary cleaning has already taken place as objects must be free from dirt, corrosion, grease, etc. before using any of these treatments.

A selection of finishing treatments.

With any treatment there is always a compromise and we should be asking what we are trying to achieve. In cleaning metal objects, while always striving to save any patina present, we will often end up stripping down to bare metal, which is not terribly attractive in many cases, particularly with copper-alloys. It is probably not a good idea to wax or lacquer anything bright and shiny unless you want to maintain the object in that state. Coin collectors tend to snub coins that have been cleaned, waxed, lacquered or messed about with in any way, so numismatically speaking, the best approach is to leave coins, which have been cleaned down to bare metal lying around in normal atmospheric conditions indefinitely, out of harm's way, to acquire a new "natural" patina. However, always keep a regular bi-monthly check on them in case corrosion re-starts.

Polishing is not recommended for antique objects, because all polishing is abrasive; however, it is widely practiced on relatively modern objects such as buttons and badges. Solvol Autosol chrome cleaner, from car accessory shops, is probably the mildest of the domestic metal polishes and conservation suppliers sell a metal polish called "Pre-Lim". For silver and silver plate, polishing cloths from jewellers or jeweller's suppliers are the least pernicious, but if using a silver polish from a supermarket etc, avoid Duraglit as it is prone to scratch. Buffing can be carried out by hand or by using a mini-drill with a rotary buffing tool.

Patination to improve the aesthetic quality of objects for display is fairly easily achievable but not necessarily desirable depending on your point of view. Conservationists would argue that it is falsifying the object's history but then so is cleaning and we are only talking of relatively mundane finds.

Richard Hughes and Michael Rowe **The Colouring, Bronzing and Patination of Metals**, is an encyclopaedic work covering hundreds of recipes which will enable you to design your own surface finish on copper-alloys and silver objects. Unfortunately, a lot of the chemicals will be very difficult to obtain, especially in small quantities and many are highly corrosive and generally nasty stuff only really suitable for laboratories and workshops; so these are not projects to be entered into lightly. However, all is not lost as there are a few readily available patinating or antiquing fluids, albeit corrosive, which I'll discuss below. One small point first is that these fluids etch the surface and if used on plated objects, may remove some or all of the plating.

Before using patinating fluids the object needs to be prepared. This involves a series of washes in various solutions. You must wear surgical gloves during this treatment, not only to protect yourself but also to protect the object from contamination from oils in the skin. Washing can be carried out by thoroughly brushing with a toothbrush or similar; soaking for 20 minutes in solution or better still, except for solvents, the indirect method in an ultrasonic cleaner, if you have one. The indirect method, you may recall, involves placing the object in solution in a small glass or plastic container within the ultrasonic tank and running the cleaner for three minutes or the normal cycle. This will remove any risk of damage to the ultrasonic cleaner and avoid the need to keep changing solutions and washing the tank out.

If the object has been previously lacquered or waxed then this has to be removed. Lacquers can usually be removed with acetone; waxes with white spirit. If the object has not been lacquered or waxed, start by washing the object with an organic solvent such as alcohol or acetone but not in an ultrasonic cleaner. The object then needs to be degreased with acid. The commercial pre-treatment is phosphoric acid based, but I would suggest 5% citric acid solution to be a suitable alternative after which the object should be washed in pure water then blotted dry with white kitchen towel.

For iron and steel you may need to rub the object with fine wire wool to remove any rust, treat with citric acid for longer, or use EDTA as an alternative acid. As results will vary from object to object it is a good idea to test an inconspicuous part first to see whether the finish is to your liking. The patination process oxidises the surface of the object, and can be removed if absolutely necessary, but will require further cleaning treatment to strip the object down to bare metal.

Liberon Antiquing Fluid (Tourmaline) is formulated to produce a black patina on bright copper-alloys but also works on silver, iron and steel. Haematite is formulated to produce a black patina on iron and steel but also works on other metals. Choose the one that best suits the metals you will treat most or both if you are patinating everything in sight!

Caution: these fluids both contain nitric acid, which will burn skin and eyeballs. Wear PVC gloves and eye protection. Apply the fluid directly onto the object with a soft brush or alternatively dilute the fluid with 10 parts water and soak. Watch the colour develop on the object, which should usually take no more than two minutes although good quality silver may take somewhat longer.

As soon as the desired colour is achieved, wash immediately with pure water and blot dry on white kitchen towel. Jade Oil is recommended to fix the patina and as a protective coating.

Scopas Cupra is formulated to produce a green patina on copper-alloys but it will also produce a copper or bronze patina on tin alloys, which is ideal for bronzing white metal replicas. This product isn't quite as nasty as the other two patinating fluids - it is only poisonous, although the safety label says wear eye protection, gloves and apron. Apply the fluid liberally and directly onto the object with a soft brush and then allow to dry. Repeat as necessary to deepen the colour. Ormoline Sealer, a resin in solvent, which gives a gloss finish, is recommended to fix the patina followed by waxing, although Jade Oil, with its moisture removing properties, should be preferable for our purposes.

Relieving is the gentle abrasion of the high points to lighten the tone or show bare metal through the patina. Traditional techniques use an artist's brush with a fine abrasive powder such as whiting or pumice powder, or a brass bristle brush; however, on most objects relieving can very easily be achieved by gently rubbing the surface with an ink eraser as discussed in mechanical cleaning. The process should be carried out immediately after patination before any surface treatment such as fixative, lacquer or wax is applied.

Jade Oil dries the surface of metals by displacing moisture and coats with a thin protective film which resists tarnishing. Caution: this fluid is flammable and may irritate the skin. Dry the object with a soft cloth or white kitchen towel. Apply the fluid to the entire surface of the object with cotton wool or a cotton bud then allow to dry for 24 hours without handling. If the object is likely to be handled frequently treat the object with Renaissance Wax for extra protection.

Incralac (INCL) is a clear glossy lacquer developed by the International Copper Research Association mainly to protect bright copper-alloys. Incralac contains 0.5% benzotriazole (BTA) as a corrosion-inhibitor and for this reason is used by conservators to coat copper-alloy objects that have been treated with BTA - protecting both the object and anyone handling the object. Incralac is available from a number of metal detector dealers and also some yacht chandlers; however, it either has to be collected or sent by road carrier as lacquers, being based on flammable solvents, are not carried by Royal Mail. You can use Incralac on any metal but if the metal hasn't been treated with solvent based BTA you will need to degrease first (wearing gloves while handling the object) by brushing with alcohol or acetone or alternatively soaking for 20 minutes. Apply incralac as evenly as possible with a soft artist's type brush, allow to dry for at least two hours, then apply a second coat. Incralac is touch dry in 15 minutes and fully cured in 2-3 days.

The problem with coatings is they are notoriously difficult to remove and you may have to remove them at some time, particularly if corrosion breaks out underneath the coating. With Incralac this is not very likely for 10 years or so; however, there is no guarantee. Incralac is xylene based and if you do need to remove the coating, xylene, which is not the easiest of solvents to get hold of, will ideally be required to remove it, although acetone will suffice.

Paraloid B72 is a clear acrylic co-polymer (plastic) widely used in conservation for lacquering all metals, particularly those having a fragile, porous or rough surface. It is available as a ready-made lacquer from conservation suppliers, with the attendant problem that Royal Mail won't carry it because of the flammability of the solvent; however, it is also available as solid granules, which Royal Mail will carry.

If you get the solid you can mix the lacquer yourself at home by dissolving 20% (20 grams in 100ml) in acetone, which you can buy in the high street. Paraloid B72 is also used in a stronger solution as a conservation adhesive, which we'll discuss later, so you can make that yourself too; you avoid any potential problems with BTA in Incralac and it is easily removed with acetone. So, if you want a more or less glossy protective coat on your metal objects and you want to avoid BTA then Paraloid B72 is the answer. You can use Paraloid B72 on any metal but if the metal hasn't been treated with solvent based BTA you will need to degrease first, wearing gloves while handling the object, by brushing with alcohol or acetone, or alternatively soaking for 20 minutes. Apply Paraloid B72 as evenly as possible with a soft artist's type brush; a second coat is not normally necessary.

Renaissance Wax (RenWax) is a blend of refined waxes to a formula used by the British Museum (and conservators world-wide) to freshen colours and protect all metal artefacts - as well as many non-metallic artefacts - giving a soft sheen to smooth surfaces.

It would be advisable to treat the object beforehand to remove moisture by brushing with alcohol or acetone or alternatively soaking for 20 minutes and allowing to dry. The wax is simply applied sparingly with a soft cloth and gently buffed. The wax dries hard instantly allowing the object to be handled without showing finger marks. Renaissance Wax can be used instead of lacquer if you prefer, and should you need to remove the wax later for further treatment, white spirit is very effective and widely available form DIY stores etc (or you can use acetone).

Microcrystalline Wax (MCW), available from some metal detector dealers, is similar to Renaissance Wax but it is used hot in its molten state. MCW can be used on all metals but its particular use is to protect and reinforce porous or cracked surfaces and is mainly used on iron objects. It would be advisable to treat the object beforehand to remove moisture by brushing with alcohol or acetone or alternatively soaking for 20 minutes and allowing to dry.

You will need a suitable heat-proof container (disposable foil containers, large enough to contain the object from pound shops etc) are ideal or you could use a metal pan, metal tongs to handle the hot object, and a heat source. Rubber gloves and covered arms would be a good idea, too, in case the hot wax splashes on you.

For small containers you can apply heat directly with a spirit lamp or tea light although it is a very slow process. It is much safer to use a water bath, particularly for treating larger objects, which could consist of a large pan of water on the stove in which you place your smaller container. You must keep the water in the pan topped up otherwise the wax could overheat and ignite; for the same reason the wax container must not be covered. If the wax does catch fire: use a powder, CO2 or foam fire extinguisher, fire-blanket or sand; not water.

Place enough solid wax pieces to cover your object in the container and set the heat source going. The wax melts at 77° C, which is rather hot although a little cooler than boiling water (100° C); however; it will burn if it splashes on your skin.

When the wax is all melted place your object in the wax using metal tongs and ensure it is fully immersed in the liquid wax, else add more

solid wax. The object, being cooler than the wax, will probably turn white as the wax solidifies on the surface. When the object has reached 77° C the wax will melt from around it and air bubbles should be seen coming from the object. When the air bubbles cease, which should be no more than an hour, the object can be removed from the wax with tongs onto white kitchen towel placed on a tray or other heat resistant surface. Surplus wax must be removed which, depending on the object, can be scraped off with a blunt knife or similar tools, or for more elaborate shapes, melted off with a hair dryer. The finished object should be lacquer coated with either Incralac or Paraloid B72. The wax can be left to cool and solidify and can be saved in the container for later reuse.

Iron cannon shot in molten Microcrystalline Wax heated in a water bath.

58

Cleaning Casebook

CM

The corrosion layer was impervious to chemical attack so barrelled with pure soap flakes for four hours, then 1.5 hours electrolysis in soda mix, with some mechanical cleaning. This nummus was fairly worn so it was finally relieved with an ink eraser.

CM

This nummus was soaked for five days in 1% citric acid solution with some mechanical cleaning. The coin is very worn so was relieved with an ink eraser.

CM

Nummus soaked in 5% citric acid for 48 hours.

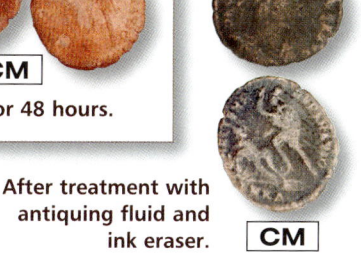

After treatment with antiquing fluid and ink eraser. CM

Nummus soaked in jeweller's stock for 24 hours followed by 1% citric acid for 24 hours.

CM

After Treatment with Scopas patinating fluid followed by relieving with ink eraser.

CM

Nummus after four hours of electrolysis followed by relieving with ink eraser.

CM

Nummus soaked in soap solution for 24 hours then four hours of electrolysis in soda mix.

CM

Nummus soaked in 5% citric acid solution for 72 hours. **CM**

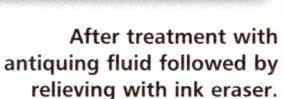

After treatment with antiquing fluid followed by relieving with ink eraser. **CM**

Nummus soaked in 10% sodium hexametaphosphate solution for five days. **CM**

13th-14th century heraldic pendant as found (left) showing traces of red enamel through dirt and corrosion. It was soaked for 21 days in pure soap solution with careful mechanical picking daily from the non-enamelled areas. Once the shield was clear the main body was brush treated with SHMP daily for seven days and then gently brushed with a glass fibre pencil. It was then soaked in water for 24 hours followed by 20 minutes in acetone; finally it was coated with Paraloid B72 lacquer (right). The arms are now identifiable as: gules, three dancets argent (three silver zig-zags on a red shield). **CM**

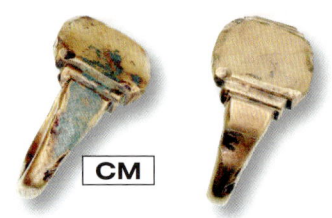

A 9 ct gold signet ring, hallmarked 1944, soaked in jeweller's stock solution for 10 minutes then buffed with soft cloth.

United States Army button before and after cleaning in jeweller's stock solution for 72 hours followed by a light brush with a brass bristle pencil.

Iron cannon shot before and after treatment with wire brush, 24 hours in EDTA, Microcrystalline Wax and Paraloid B72 lacquer.

CM

"Lead" weight before and after 24 hours in EDTA. Initial cleaning revealed a crudely engraved copper ingot under the lead corrosion. Cleaning was stopped prematurely while seeking advice.

CM

Obverse of Victoria shilling before and after cleaning with foil and sodium bicarbonate, followed by soaking for 48 hours in jeweller's stock solution.

63

Repair, Restoration & Replication

Joining

If you need to join parts of artefacts together in the way of a repair, ideally the join should be reversible so that it can be dismantled if there is an error or for some other reason. The recommended adhesives for joining metals are either Paraloid B72 or cellulose nitrate. Tubes of both adhesives are available from conservation material suppliers with the attendant problem of high transport costs mainly owing to postal regulations. We have met Paraloid B72 before in lacquer form; the adhesive version is just a lacquer with a higher concentration of solids. However, if you buy the solid and source acetone locally you can make your own adhesive as a 50% solution by dissolving 50 grams Paraloid B72 in 100ml acetone. Joins made with either adhesive can be easily taken apart by brushing acetone over the join with a fine brush.

The above adhesives do not produce strong joins; however, this is advantageous in some situations. If, for example, any stress is put on the object the join will fail. This isn't a problem for lightweight static objects, which won't be handled much. On the other hand it is not so good for anything heavy or regularly handled, or objects with moving parts; so if you need a strong joint you will have to use an epoxy adhesive suitable for joining metals, such as the widely available Araldite. Just make sure you get the join right first time, as it could prove impossible to dismantle.

Restoration

With the will and resource it should be possible to restore, or return to near original condition, almost anything. However, restoration projects can consume a great deal of time and money and you should seriously consider whether the end result will be worth the effort or even desirable. Conservators of archaeological artefacts rarely attempt to restore to "as new" condition because it may not be aesthetically pleasing and in many cases the precise new condition is unknown. On the other hand, you may gain a great deal of pleasure in taking a wreck from the more recent past and re-fashioning it into an object that you can display with pride. Of course, there are potentially as many restoration projects as there are broken artefacts (or "partefacts" as they are popularly called) and to try and cover even a representative range could take several volumes. Therefore I'm just going to briefly discuss a couple of examples as a taster.

A good few years ago I found part of a small pistol which looked pretty old.

Having little knowledge of antique firearms I took it to a local gunsmith, who identified it as a Continental box-lock, probably Belgian, pocket or lady's muff pistol c.1790. I then asked about restoration. To this the gentleman replied that there were certainly experts who could do the job; however, the problem was that it would cost a lot more than the restored pistol would be worth. The part I had, though, was worth only a few pounds as it stood. The other possibility was a DIY job, by either sourcing replica parts (that were apparently readily available at the time) or making parts from scratch. I must have mentioned my "O" level in metalwork and access to engineering facilities I had through my employment, for the gentleman kindly sketched out all the missing parts for me and wished me good luck.

The first thing I did was to go through my junk and scrap boxes in case I had already found non-ferrous parts of pistols and not recognised them. Unfortunately, this was not the case so my next step, with sketch in hand, was to discuss the project with a friendly professional engineer who basically explained that I would have to carve all the main parts from lumps of solid metal. This would be not quite as easy as is whittling wood! An alternative would have been to sculpt patterns from easily worked materials and cast the parts in soft metal. However, that would have only produced a static model on account of the low strength of the castings and I really wanted an authentic pistol.

I therefore set about making the parts during my lunch breaks at work. Both the top plate and bottom strap were fairly easy to make as brass is relatively soft. The hammer was really tricky as it started out as a solid cube of steel and while some of the waste could be drilled and sawn away the main part had to be rounded and needed hours of filing to get the shape correct. The springs were fashioned from an old clock mainspring. I did have some help with some of the parts: the gunsmith provided the percussion nipple; a blacksmith brazed the bottom strap on to the box and shaped the curves in the top plate and trigger guard; an instrument engineer lathe-turned the two pivots and a wood-turner carved the stock. To finish off, the steel parts were treated with antiquing fluid followed by jade oil and renaissance wax. The whole project took two years to complete and consumed over 100 hours of work - but I am well pleased with the result.

Firearms represent one group of objects where replica parts can be obtained or made; timepieces are another and die-cast models yet another - although all will need plenty of patience to get back into working order.

The next project, though, is much less ambitious and involves restoring a Henry III penny. This, however, was not only broken but had a piece missing. While not exactly a modern item, this coin is far from being unique and has almost nil value as a collector's item.

Because the adhesive and filler would stick the coin onto whatever surface it was placed on, I started with a small flat piece of silicon release paper (the backing for self adhesive labels etc). If you don't have any release paper you can use plain white paper and give it a smooth coating of washable adhesive like PVA and allow to dry. A paper glue stick is ideal for this.

Place the coin on the paper and carefully stick the two broken parts together using Paraloid B72 or cellulose nitrate adhesive and leave to set. Coat the edges of the gap with Paraloid B72 lacquer, as a separating layer, and leave to set. The gap can now be filled carefully with a two-part plastic filler such as Plastic Padding, David's Isopon or epoxy putty. The fillers are grey to green in colour, whereas epoxy putty comes in a range of colours: black, white, grey, silver, terracotta, copper, etc. For my small coin I used Plastic Padding and applied it with a cocktail stick. If you have the coin displayed side up you can add a complementary pattern before the filler hardens if you wish. As the filler was hardening I trimmed the uneven edge with a scalpel. Leave the repair to harden then carefully peel off the paper; if the paper is stuck firmly, soak the paper off by immersing in water with the paper uppermost until it floats off. Tidy up the filled part as necessary with needle files, nail files or wet and dry paper (used wet) and wrapped around a paintbrush handle or similar, depending on the size of the repair. The restored area can be painted to match the rest of the object as necessary. (Using Humbrol enamel model paints, I painted the restored area silver.) Finally dry off in alcohol (not acetone or the joins will fall apart) and coat with Paraloid B72 lacquer.

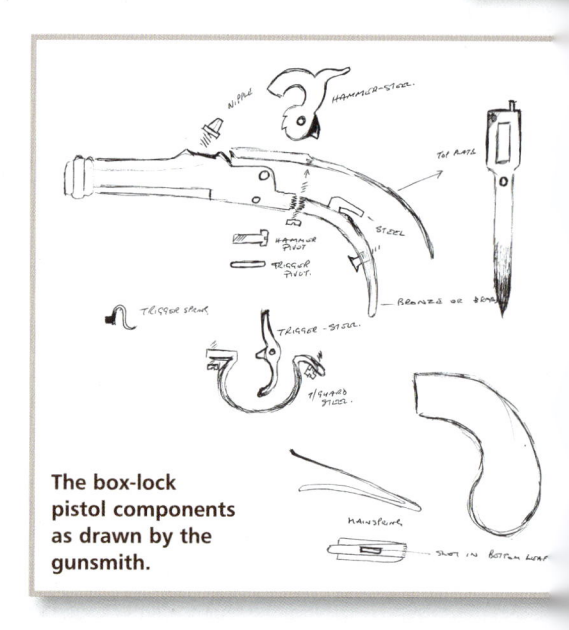

The pistol barrel and box as found (after cleaning by barrelling).

The box-lock pistol components as drawn by the gunsmith.

The restored pistol.

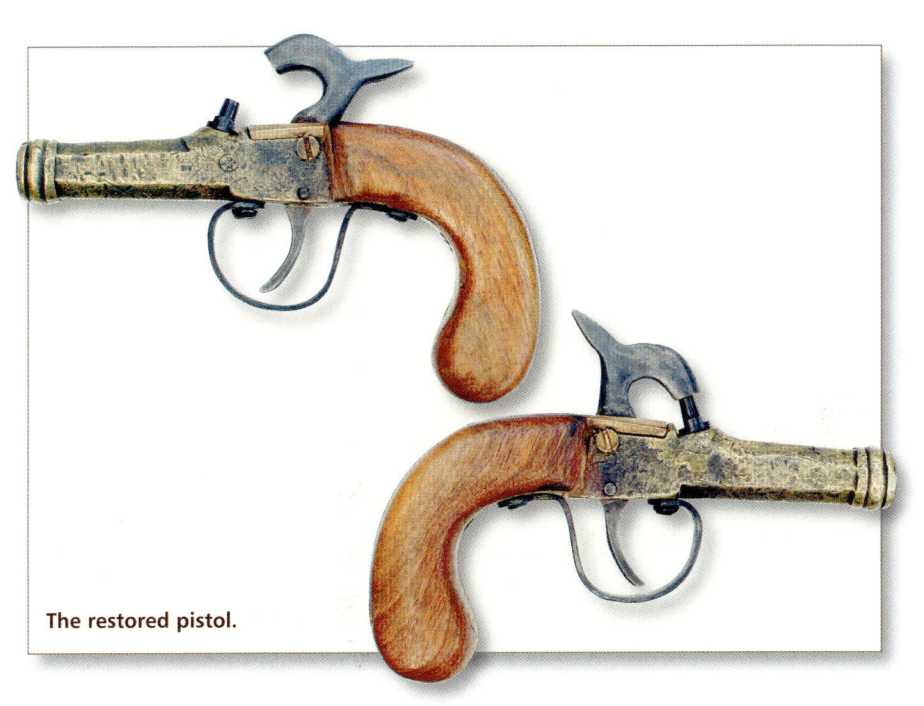

Henry III silver penny before and after cleaning and restoration. The coin was cleaned using aluminium foil and sodium bicarbonate.

Reshaping

The conservator's view seems to be that any damage to an object is part of its history and is best left alone. I have some sympathy for this view, particularly if it is reasonable to assume the object has been deliberately damaged such as the bending of coins into love tokens. If the object has merely lost an argument with a plough, then I think it is a candidate for reshaping providing its original shape is definitely known. The next problem is that many objects crack or break when put under the stresses of reshaping, so careful consideration needs to be given to the real possibility that you'll have two partefacts instead of one object and whether you'll be able to either fix or live with that. For any potentially valuable object the best course is to employ the hard-earned skills of a professional restorer or independent jeweller, for the rest we need to proceed cautiously with this one and look at one metal at a time.

Gold is probably the only relatively frequently found metal that can be reshaped cold without too much risk (providing it is not too badly misshapen). However, as all gold objects will be relatively valuable, I have so far resisted the do-it-yourself route. If you are brave enough to try reshaping yourself then follow the guidelines for silver as most gold objects will be alloyed with either silver or copper to form a more economical yet harder wearing alloy.

I have only had two gold objects reshaped, both by a local independent jeweller. The first was an Edward III quarter noble, which was bent almost double on recovery. The jeweller basically used a rawhide mallet and block of smooth hardwood to hammer the coin out flat. He did say you needed to stop hammering before the design started to flatten out too.

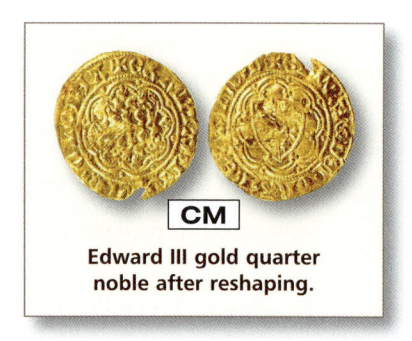

Edward III gold quarter noble after reshaping.

The second object was a 17th century *memento mori* ring that I had reported under the Treasure Act but was subsequently disclaimed and returned to me. It was in quite a sorry state, being twisted as well as oval in shape, and full of dents, nicks, scratches and gouges.

The jeweller put it on a mandrel and set about it with his rawhide mallet and returned it to ring shape. The surface indentations are still there as one option was to try and fill the blemishes; but there was little chance of matching the colour. Another option, which I rejected, was to grind the surface down and end up with a much slimmer ring.

Memento mori ring before and after restoration.

Silver that is only moderately distorted can usually be reshaped cold with care; that is, providing it is relatively pure. Silver is usually alloyed with copper and very debased silver containing a high amount of copper will need to be treated as a copper-alloy. Thin section objects like slightly bent hammered silver coins can be straightened using a pair of ordinary (combination) pliers but protect the object by wrapping either the nose of the pliers, or the part of the object to be gripped, with a layer of chamois leather. Chamois leathers can be bought from places like hardware stores, or motor accessory shops and you can save some money if

68

you buy the reclaimed type consisting of small pieces sewn together.

Once you have the object roughly reshaped with pliers there will probably be ridges and bumps left. Place the object ridges and bumps upward on a smooth hard surface such as Formica or steel, so that the object can slide (otherwise the edges of the coin may dig in and cause the coin to break). You can then work the dents and creases out by pressing on them with your fingers or wooden tools, such as dowels and clothes pegs covered with chamois. In fact, if you wish, you can carry out the entire reshaping of an object with fingers and chamois covered wooden tools on a smooth hard surface.

Slightly bent and creased Elizabeth I sixpence before and after reshaping.

If the object is badly misshapen (ie the bends in it are greater than 20 degrees), then you really need to try and soften the silver first by a process called annealing. In theory you heat the object up in a flame, such as a gas hob or blow-lamp, until it glows red and then let it cool. However, this might make an awful mess of your treasured object as corrosion products can melt or burn-up at much lower temperatures, leaving lumps or pitting respectively.

The best approach to annealing is to heat the silver object in a domestic oven at full heat for two hours. Then remove the object with metal tongs and place on a heatproof surface to cool. You should then be able to reshape the object (by no more than 20 degrees at a time) before it work hardens and goes brittle. If more reshaping is required, you would need to repeat the annealing process.

Lead should respond reasonably well to cold reshaping with little other than the fingers. This may result in surface cracks but you should be able to deal with that by treating with lacquer or microcrystalline wax, if necessary. Also, be aware that lead objects, such as seals and tokens, have designs which may become distorted during reshaping. Tin and lead alloys like pewter tend to be very brittle and so far as reshaping is concerned are best either left alone, or passed on to a professional conservator.

Copper-alloys will usually crack or break if reshaping is attempted, even if they are annealed. However, thin section objects offer the best chance of success using the reshaping techniques discussed under silver. You are unlikely to reshape any copper-alloy object cold, so - using metal tongs - it will need to be heated up in a flame to red heat and then quenched in a metal container of cold water to soften it. This is different to silver, although base silver will respond to annealing in this way owing to the copper content. The heating process will blacken the surface and may burn-up corrosion products, thus causing pitting; so you'll have to undertake more cleaning of the object afterwards. If you must try to reshape heavier objects, then squeezing in a vice (protect the object from the jaws with rubber or chamois), hammering a block of chamois covered wood, a rawhide hammer or a rubber hammer against the bend might succeed.

Iron that has been corroding in the ground will be extremely fragile and again likely to break. To anneal iron you use the same technique as silver, which is to heat to red heat in a flame, remove with metal tongs and place on a heatproof surface to cool. Reshaping treatment will take the form of vice or hammer previously ascribed to copper-alloys. The heating process will scar the surface more than with copper-alloys so you'll likely have extensive surface treatment to carry out afterwards.

Replication

The first time I had a need to replicate an object was when I found a 15th-16th century gold iconographic ring. The ring was reported as potential Treasure, of course, but before it had even got that far both the landowner and my wife had laid claim to it. I knew that once I handed the ring in for Treasure I would not be able to have the ring, whatever happened. If a museum didn't want it I would have to let the landowner take it.

I needed a replica and I wanted an authentic replica in gold, so before I handed the ring in, I took it to my local independent jeweller and asked if he could make a copy. "No problem", he said and made a mould from the ring. He then took some scrap 22 carat gold wedding rings, which were the closest match for colour, and made a duplicate. There was a slight problem, however, which we were aware of from the outset. The casting material, having to withstand very high temperatures from molten gold, did not reproduce the finer detail and the casting had to be sent to a specialist engraver to replicate the design from photographs.

The engraving did take some while, but eventually was completed and matched the original well. I was planning to have the ring hallmarked to differentiate it from the original but, with my wife's birthday looming, I ran out of time and settled for a modern inscription inside the hoop instead. As it happened, the original ring was declared Treasure and now resides in a local museum. My half of the award covered the cost of the replica almost 10 times over.

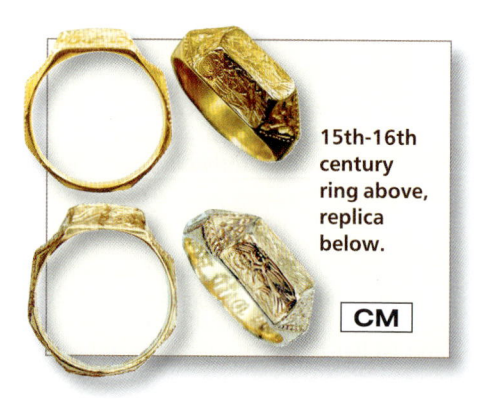

15th-16th century ring above, replica below.

CM

Keeping a loved one happy is a very good reason to produce a replica but others are to:-

* Share an object with the landowner and others

* Protect valuable objects from excessive handling, deterioration, theft, etc

* Make replacement parts for partefacts

* Reversibly restore a partefact (ie temporarily restore an object so it can be replicated complete)

* Sell (have your cake and eat it).

I am not suggesting you cast replicas in gold or any other metal that originals are made from. However, there are excellent low melting point alloys and suitable mould making materials, which anyone may use to make convincing replicas. These replicas are so convincing that it is advisable to apply a letter "R" to them with a tool punch to distinguish them from the real thing. You don't even have to do the job yourself as detectorist Brian Cross has a company, Museum Reproductions, making such things. He will sometimes even make replicas for nothing if he wants to add your object to his list.

However, if you want to make replicas yourself it isn't difficult; but you will need quite a few items, so the best way to start is to buy a kit.

The object to be replicated will need to be clean, dry and free from flaking patina as much as possible. Therefore wash in soap solution followed by pure water, and degrease with alcohol or acetone as a minimum. You do not need to lacquer your object but it will aid release and protect the object if you do. You may need or want to carry out temporary or even permanent repairs first, so you really need to consider how your original object is going to be left after the mould making. If you want your object "as is" then lacquer it with Paraloid B72 before any reconstruction (which you will also have to lacquer); then wash everything off with acetone after you have made the mould. If you want your object left reconstructed then any

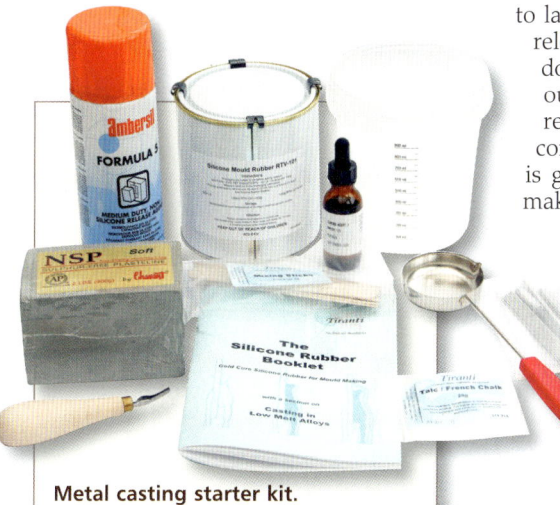

Metal casting starter kit.

lacquering can be done last. Bear in mind that you do need to treat the object with acetone or alcohol before applying lacquer and to wear gloves otherwise you may end up with fingerprints reproduced on your replicas.

We have already covered repairs but if the "repair" is only to be temporary until the mould has been made, then care will be needed throughout. Any of the materials discussed such as Plastic Padding or epoxy putty can be used, but other materials such as modelling clay, modelling or encaustic wax or even plasticine are quite suitable for temporary repairs. Remember to blend in the finish on the repair to match that on the rest of the object (ie if the object is pitted, the repair should also imitate pitting). Once you are satisfied with the overall result allow the repair to dry and apply lacquer as required (20% Paraloid B72 in acetone recommended).

As the metal used for casting has a low melting point, a flexible mould can be made of heat and shrinkage resistant silicone rubber. Moulds can be made quickly and easily with excellent definition that can produce very intricate castings owing to their flexibility. There are several types of silicone rubber and several suppliers. I am using mainly RTV-101 for moulds of fairly simple shape without any deep cavities and T20 for complex shapes and deep cavities or undercutting. Alec Tiranti Limited supplies both.

As silicone rubbers cure by catalytic action, the thickness of the mould is largely immaterial. The approximate cure time of RTV-101 is between 5.5 hours and 24 hours (T20 2-5 hours), depending on the temperature and the amount of catalyst used. Once cured, the moulds should ideally be left exposed to air for 48 hours before initial use; this allows time for solvents to completely evaporate.

The simplest mould to make is one-piece but your object will need to be uni-face to take advantage of this. Always check your object over with a magnifying glass to ensure it is scrupulously clean before you make your mould. To make the mould, place the object in a box or frame, ideally made from a suitably-sized base of a flat sheet of cardboard, thin metal, plastic or wood, with sides built of Lego bricks (the bottom row of which can be stuck firmly to the base with double-sided adhesive tape). The rubber solution will not flow through the joints in the bricks providing they are pressed tightly together. If the kids won't let you borrow their bricks, you can use cardboard, thin metal, plastic or wood for the sides, which can be attached to the base and held together with adhesive tape or modelling clay. Allow at least a 7mm or 0.25 inches clearance between the object and the sides of the mould.

If your object is lacquered you should not need a release agent for a one-piece mould; however, to be on the safe side you can use a purpose made release agent aerosol sprayed-on from 25-30cm (10-12 inches) away. Alternatively 5% petroleum jelly (Vaseline) (5 grams in 100ml white spirit) can be used, although it is less easy to apply. It will be beneficial to treat the base and sides of the mould-box with release agent as well as the object.

For my one-piece mould I am replicating the pin from a ring buckle in order to repair a contemporary silver-gilt ring brooch missing its pin. As I would have to damage the buckle to remove the pin I have set the entire buckle into modelling clay to obtain a flat surface on the underside of the pin.

One-piece mould ready for rubber solution.

The next thing is to make up the rubber solution, which comes in two parts: the rubber and catalyst or hardener (curing agent). While it is not rocket science, for best results the rubber and catalyst should be measured out fairly accurately. I suggest you wear gloves and protect surfaces with plenty of newspaper or kitchen towel as the process is inclined to be a bit messy. It is fairly simple to use a small plastic food container on kitchen scales to weigh out the rubber solution but remember to either "tare" (zero) the scales with the empty container in place or deduct the weight of the container. You can calculate how much solution you will need by measuring the mould in centimetres and multiplying width x depth x length to arrive at the volume in cubic centimetres (cc) or millilitres (ml).

There is the added complication that the specific gravity of rubber solution is around 1.5, depending on the grade, so 100mls will weigh 150 grams. Before adding the two parts together, it is essential that the rubber and catalyst are both well mixed independently. Then the catalyst is added drop-wise to the rubber from a dropper bottle and thoroughly mixed - either by hand or using a mechanical stirrer. We are now ready to make the mould.

Stand the mould-box on a firm level surface. Start by brushing a layer of rubber solution onto the object, especially if it is intricate or has cavities, which will help avoid air bubbles forming. Pour the rubber solution slowly into a corner of the box, allowing it to flow over and around the object. Stop pouring when the object is half-covered and allow a few minutes for the solution to level itself. Continue pouring until at least 7mm or 0.25 inches of rubber solution covers the highest point of the object and leave to cure.

One-piece mould.

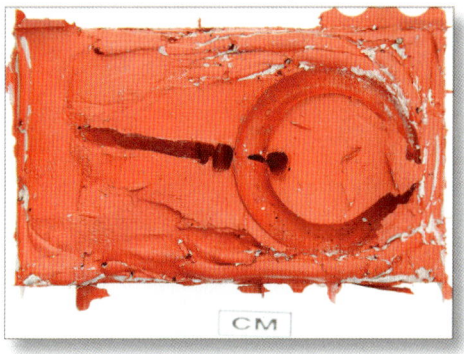

73

To make two-sided and three-dimensional castings, you'll need a two-piece mould. Using a rolling-pin or similar, roll out some fairly soft synthetic modelling clay large enough to cover a suitably-sized working area on a flat piece of board until it is flat and about the same thickness as the object.

To avoid problems in making and curing the mould, it is important that the modelling clay is sulphur-free and non-drying such as NSP by Chavant. Brush on a very thin layer of talc over the area where the object will be placed, usually in the middle; also brush talc on the object to avoid it sticking to the modelling clay. Decide where you want your dividing line, which should be in a place it will be noticed least. Place the object in the modelling clay and gently press until roughly half of the object is buried. Now build a box around the object as before, using a suitable material such as Lego bricks, thin metal, plastic, wood, etc. Allow 7-13mm (0.25-0.5 inches) clearance between the object and the walls of the mould. Push a small ball bearing or dowel half way into the modelling clay in each corner, and half way along one side, to form registration holes. Alternatively, carve small trenches or construct small cones or ridges in the clay across each corner and half way along one side so that the two halves of the mould will fit together accurately and only one-way.

Spray or brush release the agent gently and thinly over every surface inside the mould-box, including the object and walls and allow it to dry. Start by brushing a layer of rubber solution onto the object, especially if it is intricate or has cavities, which will help avoid air bubbles forming. Pour the rubber solution slowly into a corner of the box, allowing it to flow over and around the object. Stop pouring when the object is half-covered and allow a few minutes for the solution to level itself. Continue pouring until at least 7mm or 0.25 inches of rubber solution covers the highest point of the object and leave to cure.

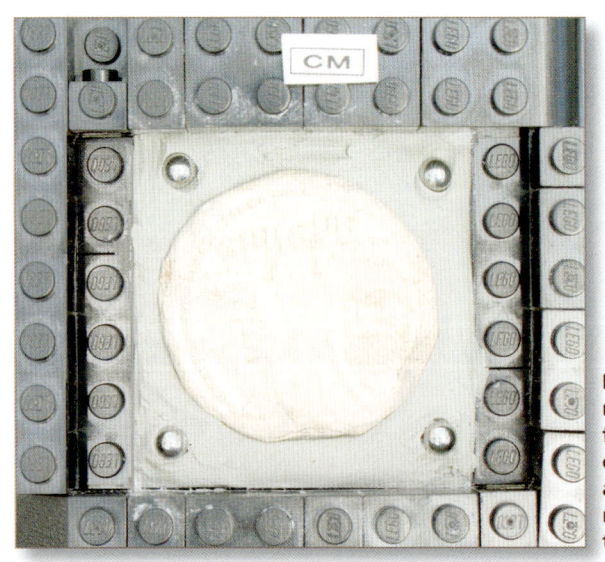

First half of two-piece mould of Papal Bulla ready for rubber solution. I have expanded the mould by half a brick each side to allow room for vents to be put in the mould later.

74

First half of mould completed and ready for pouring second half.

mould or you will disturb the release layer and have difficulties separating the two halves of the mould later. Pour the rubber solution slowly into a corner of the box, allowing it to flow over and around the object. Stop pouring when the object is half-covered and allow a few minutes for the solution to level itself. Continue pouring until at least 7mm or 0.25 inches of rubber solution covers the highest point of the object and leave to cure.

To make the second half of the mould, remove the box from the cured half mould and, without removing the object from the mould, gently extract both from the modelling clay. Ensure there is no modelling clay sticking to the object and clean it as necessary. Invert the mould so the object is face up and replace the box around ensuring any gaps are suitably sealed. Also, remove any ball bearings or dowels that may have stuck in the rubber. Spray or brush release agent gently and thinly over every surface inside the mould-box, including the object and walls and allow it to dry.

Start by brushing a layer of rubber solution onto the object as before, but ensure that you don't brush the rubber

Once cured the box can be removed, the two halves of the mould parted and the object extracted. Taking a scalpel or sharp craft knife, carefully cut a tapered pour hole at the top of both sides of the mould. As this type of casting is known as gravity casting it is important to make the pour hole large enough to accommodate sufficient metal to force it into the mould and force out gases through the vent holes. Also, using a sprue cutter or V shaped cutter, cut two thin vent holes, one on each side of one half of the mould, with branches at the base, and one-third and two-thirds up the object, to allow gases to escape from the molten metal. Keep these fairly small to begin with, as they can always be enlarged later if necessary.

75

The two halves of the finished mould. The pouring and vent holes have been outlined in white.

When you are ready to make a casting, the inside of your mould should be brushed lightly with talc or graphite powder. The two halves of a two-piece mould should be banged together to get rid of excess powder, and then held together using a clamp. Two pieces of hardboard are then placed on either side of mould to help to keep the mould stable and clamping pressure even. The mould should be stood securely upright on a heat resistant tray or similar, to avoid any spillage on to work surfaces etc.

There is a range of casting alloys available and you can even use scrap pewter that you find (but make sure it is scrap!) The metal that I am using to melt down and fill the mould is a lead-bismuth alloy of the type supplied with the starter kit. It gives excellent detail with a matt finish, has a melting point of 168° C and is ready for pouring at between 220° C and 230° C. Pewter, on the other hand, is lead free and very rich in tin - giving a highly detailed finish, which can be polished to a high sheen similar to silver. Pewter has a melting point of 245° C and is ready for pouring at between 280° C and 300° C.

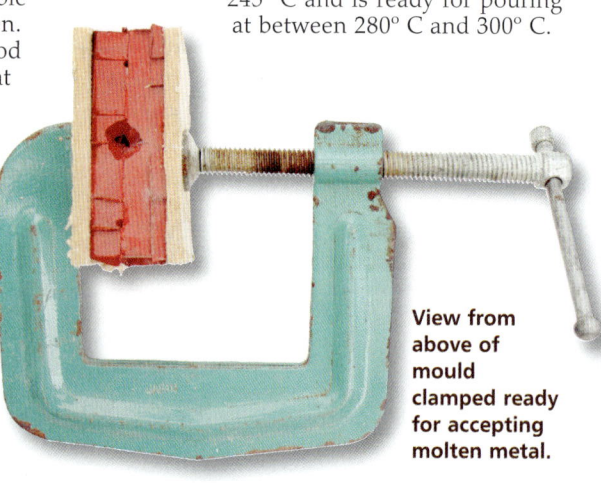

View from above of mould clamped ready for accepting molten metal.

76

Remember that you are using a very hot metal and take care! Wear gloves and goggles and do not allow molten metal to come into contact with water. You will need a flat-bottomed ladle to melt the metal in, which is placed over a ring on an ordinary domestic gas cooker or picnic stove etc. This is heated up until a spent matchstick or cocktail stick, placed in the ladle with the metal, just begins to smoke. Pour the molten metal in one steady continuous easy stream and tap the mould lightly to allow the metal to fill the whole of the mould.

You will probably be able to produce around 1000 castings from one mould, if you wish. With practice you will be able to turn out casts very quickly; however, do not allow the mould to get too hot or if it does allow it to cool for a few minutes.

Now you have successfully made your casting it is necessary to finish it to give the desired effect. Firstly, snip off any excess metal from the pour hole and vents using a small pair of suitable pliers or pincers. Lightly file these areas using a needle file or similar. If you have cast anything with a hole through, the hole will need to be filed and in some cases drilled through.

Of course, the casting will be bright and shiny and silver coloured, so if the object wasn't silver or white metal you can use Liberon Antiquing Fluid for a grey to black finish or Scopas Cupra for a bronze finish on tin alloys as discussed under Finishing Treatments.

CM

The cast replica Papal Bulla of Nicholas IV.

CM

Silver-gilt ring brooch as found and fitted with cast replica pin.

77

Photographing Your Finds

For traditional or film cameras the only suitable type of camera is a single lens reflex (SLR), where viewing is directly through the lens. Non SLR or compact cameras use a viewfinder, which is fine for shots at a reasonable distance but hopeless for extremely close photography of small objects or macro photography. The main problem is that you cannot line up the object with the lens, with a secondary problem that you cannot easily change the focal length of the lens. Anyway if you want a SLR film camera, they are now available very cheaply on the second-hand market and a new entry-level camera can be bought for less then £100.

Film is required for traditional cameras, of course, and the options are becoming limited owing to the success of digital cameras; most film is of the fast daylight type. I like to use a slower film to enable more light to get into the camera and try and keep within the range 100-200 ISO. When I was using mostly film for finds photography, I found the mail order processing services like Truprint, which gave a free replacement film, to be very cost effective.

The essential capability to focus within a few centimetres of the object can be achieved with either a macro lens, which replaces the normal lens, or extension tubes, which fit between the camera body and the lens. A macro lens is more expensive but less of a fiddle; however, the choice is yours or may be made for you depending on what is available.

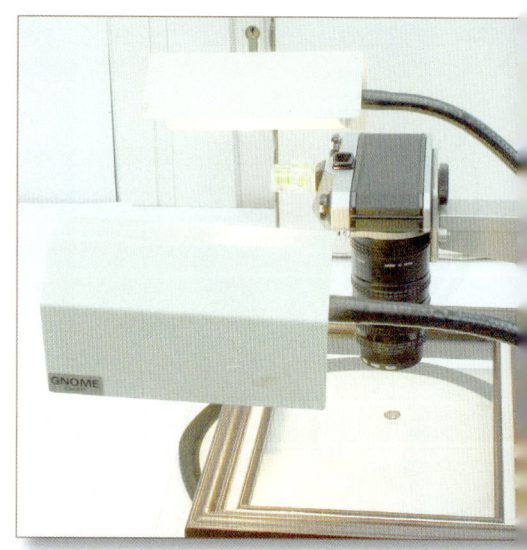

Asahi Pentax K1000 film SLR camera fitted with set of three extension tubes and on copy stand.

Digital cameras are now so well advanced that almost any camera will be able to take good photographs of small objects, the main exception being most mobile telephone cameras. SLR digital cameras are available, with the same advantages of control as film SLRs in that you can change lenses, fit filters and manually focus; however, they are expensive and only really necessary if you are taking photographs professionally. Point and shoot digital cameras allow viewing through the lens, by using the camera's LCD screen, so you can see the object you are photographing. However, these screens are relatively low resolution so you may not be able to tell whether a small object is in focus, even if the camera has a manual focus facility. But auto-focus systems are accurate much of the time and you can usually enlarge the image on the screen enough to determine the focus. If it is out of focus you can just delete and retake the shot.

Canon EOS 350D SLR digital camera with macro lens on copy stand.

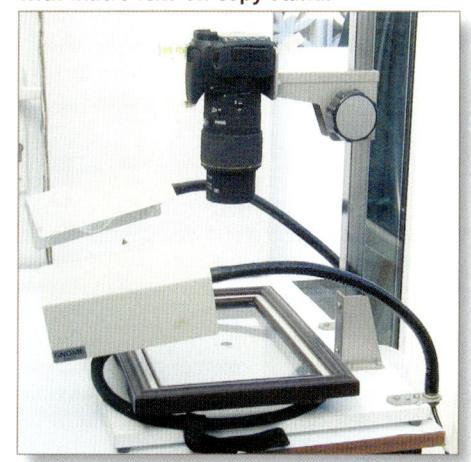

The other consideration with digital cameras is resolution, which is measured in megapixels, a pixel being the smallest piece of information in an image or a tiny dot of colour. The digital equivalent resolution to standard film is three megapixels so anything above that, which is the norm these days, will produce an image better than film provided the camera has a good quality lens. However, digital cameras down to one megapixel can produce quite satisfactory close up images so don't throw that old camera out yet. Your camera will also need to have a zoom or macro facility or be capable of focusing very close to the object, ideally within 10cm or 4 inches.

Most digital cameras have a zoom facility but in some cameras this is a digital zoom, which just blows-up the image and in so doing reduces resolution so you effectively reduce the megapixel rating using this mode. This is fine so long as you have oodles of megapixels to play with. An optical zoom is much better, where the lens physically moves out from the camera body to magnify the image. If you are buying a new digital camera for photographing finds, try and check it out in the shop on a small object, before you buy.

Having sorted out the camera, we then need to securely fix it to enable precise close-up shots and minimise vibration or "camera-shake" as it is called. The two options are basically a tripod or copy stand. Tripods are generally cheaper than copy stands and may give more options for other photographic tasks. If using a tripod you need to consider where the object is going to be placed as standard-sized tripods have relatively long legs that tend to get in the way. However, you will probably be able to stand the object on a stack of books, for example, to bring it nearer the camera. There are mini tripods available and also small table clamp tripods, which clamp on to the edge of a table or desk, allowing you to place the object on the tabletop or on a suitable plinth to the side.

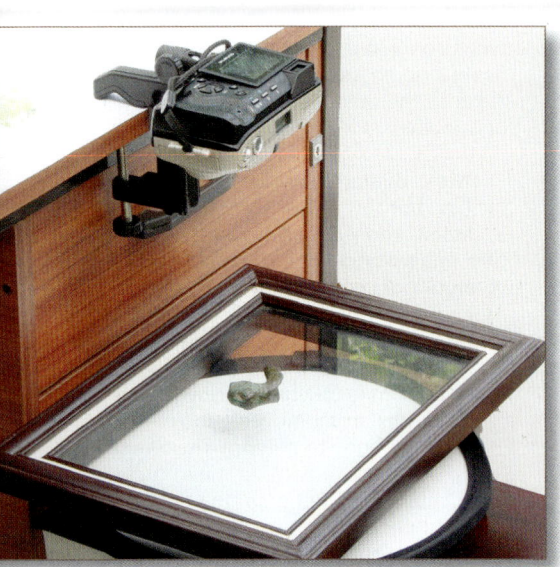

some finds photographers have a small lightweight board fitted onto the tripod centre column below the camera upon which to place the object. You can make this yourself by attaching an L-bracket to a piece of rigid board, up to about 12 inches (305mm) square, then use a U-bolt or exhaust clamp to attach that securely to the tripod centre column.

Olympus D-490 zoom compact digital camera (2.1 megapixel) fitted to table clamp tripod. (Note: These tripods will not support the heavier SLR cameras).

Fixing arrangement on underside of tripod table, size 210mm (8.3 inches) x 160mm (6.3 inches).

Some tripods have reversible centre columns so you can move the camera closer to the floor or whatever surface the tripod stands on. While, I have not seen them available commercially,

The camera also needs to be level, both horizontally and vertically otherwise your object will be, at best, only partly in focus. This is less of a problem with copy stands than tripods as stands are fixed precisely in the vertical position so you only need to level your camera in the horizontal plane. You can set your camera up using a spirit level; in fact, you can buy spirit levels that fit on to the camera's hot shoe, if it has one.

Canon DSLR with standard lens on tripod with table fitted.

An alternative is to use a plumb-line to set your camera's level up.

One other consideration regarding fixing the camera to a tripod or copy stand is that the tripod mounting point on the base of the camera should ideally be central. Some cameras have the mounting point offset to one side of the base and because the camera isn't supported from below in our application, gravity allows the camera to creep out of parallel with the object.

If your camera has the facility for a cable release to operate the shutter remotely, then using a cable release will eliminate any shake that may be caused when operating the camera hands on. An alternative is to use the delay timer, if fitted, which will allow any shake set up, when the shutter button was pressed, to subside before the shot is taken.

We are not quite ready to start taking photos yet, as there are a few more items

we need to consider. Firstly, something to lay the find on. There is often a problem of shadow being cast by the angle of light falling on the object, which tends to obscure the detail on part of the edge. One remedy is to place the object on a dark background where any shadow disappears into the background; however, this is not very acceptable if the picture is going to be offered for publication as **Treasure Hunting** along with some other publishers, prefer a white background (to allow for easier "cutting out" of the object from its background on computer). The best option is to place the object on a sheet of glass or clear plastic supported on blocks at the corners or in a frame; this allows the shadows to basically disappear below the glass and away from the object. It works even better if you place a white disc reflector below the glass, which not only helps fade the shadows but reflects more light into the lens (a boon for film cameras which can use only a fraction of the available light that digital cameras can use).

If you are taking photographs for publication or identification it is essential to show a scale in your shot; in fact, it is good practice to show a scale regardless of the end use of your photographs. It's clumsy in my opinion but a simple way is to photograph a well-known modern coin alongside the object. But use coins that haven't changed in size during their life like (currently) 1p, 2p and 20p pieces and have the value side facing the camera. Another way is to use a rule ensuring you get the name of the units in the photograph or you can buy or make up scales, basically consisting of alternating light and dark rectangles, each representing a centimetre, for instance; but the unit of measurement should always be included. **Treasure Hunting** magazine favours a simple one or two unit rectangle, for small and larger objects respectively, containing the letters CM for centimetre. Below are some that you can photocopy, then cut out and use.

The next consideration is lighting. Natural daylight is the most easily obtained light source for taking photographs. Unfortunately, any old daylight won't quite do. The optimum conditions are light cloud cover with the sun low in the sky as in early morning or early evening. Avoid strong sunlight, which tends to cause excessive contrast and heavily overcast, wet or foggy days, which cause lack of contrast. Lighting should always be shining from in front or to the side of the object; lighting from behind will reverse the image so high spots look low and vice-versa.

To accompany small objects.

To accompany large objects

When daylight isn't available you can still take photographs but avoid using the camera's flash, as you will often get bright spots from the reflection. You can take photographs under tungsten light but the photographs will have an orange tinge unless you fit a daylight correction filter to the lens or use tungsten film in traditional cameras. If you take photographs under fluorescent light, of which, unlike tungsten, there are many types, they will usually have a green tinge unless you fit a suitable correction filter. With digital cameras you should be able to correct the colour balance with the software but it is probably easier to get it right in the first place. Alternatively you can use daylight lamps to provide the lighting; two 100 watt lamps, one either side of the object should be quite adequate.

Now we have all the technology sorted we just have to plan our photographs and take them. The set of photographs should show all the detail necessary so that anyone looking at them can understand the object as if they were actually handling it, although in practice a few words of text describing metal of manufacture and weight would obviously help.

Some objects, such as buckles are clearly uniface, so unless there is a reverse design or inscription, a front view only would be quite sufficient. Coins, tokens and similar paranumismatica have at least an obverse and reverse so would require a photograph of each side at least (even uniface staters) and the right way up wherever possible. Some coins and paranumismatica have an edge inscription, which would require several more photographs to cover that aspect. Most three-dimensional objects would need at least front, reverse and side views; possibly a top and bottom view also. To achieve some of these photographs the object may need supporting and in some cases levelling to keep essential details in the same plane and in focus; a crotal bell can be photographed with its loop horizontal, for instance. Blu-Tack will serve this purpose although you should endeavour to keep it hidden and it must be removed completely immediately following the photograph session as it may leave harmful deposits.

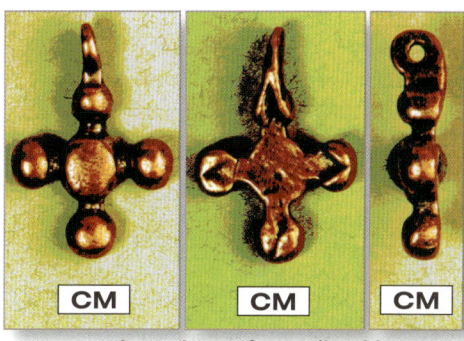

Three views of a medieval horse harness pendant.

When it comes to actually taking the picture it is important that the object fills as much of the frame as possible, apart from leaving a small margin all round to avoid the risk of chopping off part of the object. Where you have control of the aperture setting this should be as near minimum as possible, which is the highest number (ie f22 to give the greatest depth of field). Getting sufficient light into the camera is a big problem for film cameras so use the lowest shutter speed (ie 1 second and if you can adjust the light meter settings then set it one or two stops over-exposed to the + side). There is an acceptable compromise here in that you will have to increase the aperture to let more light in, if you cannot reduce the shutter speed further. Focus carefully and accurately and use a cable-release or the camera's delay timer to steady the camera and you should have great photographs.

I'm just going to say a little about photo-editing programs of which there are a considerable number. Most digital cameras come with their own photo-editing software or you may prefer to use popular programs like Adobe Photoshop, Corel Paint Shop Pro or the free Gimp (www.gimp.org). Basically the software lets you alter your digital photos or scanned prints, slides and negatives, to your liking. Common features include brightness and contrast enhancement, colour changes, cropping and cloning. The crop tool lets you select an area to retain while losing the remainder and the clone tool enables you to copy an area and paste it elsewhere, which is very useful when you find unwanted specks or shadows in your picture. Other useful features include mirroring which is ideal for imitating a seal impression from a matrix; stitching, which allows you to make several photographs into one and image sizing so you can make your photograph suitable for a range of applications. *(Please note: if supplying photographs for publication, most magazines/book publishers prefer "un-tampered" images and to make any necessary corrections themselves).*

14th century copper-alloy seal matrix with mirror image on right.

Saxon horse harness cheek piece fragment reconstructed with photo-editing software below.

I am not a great fan of scanning objects probably because my all-in-one Brother scanner-printer isn't that good at the task on three-dimensional objects, although some scanners can achieve an image quality rivalling top of the range digital cameras.

Before you scan the object, check that the scanner's glass bed is clean and free from dust. Use a glass or VDU cleaner if necessary. You will only be able to close the scanner cover on thin objects like coins; however, this will produce an undesirable shadow so leave the lid up and have a reasonable level of lighting in the room. If your scanner will produce good images of 3D objects, bear in mind that scanners work upside down compared to cameras and if any support is required it has to be from above the object. Use a suitably sized clear plastic container and pack the object up with Blu-Tack, modelling clay, etc - so that it is level and flush with the rim of the container - then invert the container on the scanner bed. Remove all the packing material from the object as soon as you have finished your scanning session.

To scan your object, place it on the scanner bed with a suitable scale all correctly orientated. I like to scan directly into my photo-editing software; alternatively you can either press the scan button on your scanner or open your scanner software. In my scanner software, I select photo and the highest resolution, which is 600 x 600 dpi and document size as business card or as appropriate if the object is large.

I then use pre-scan (preview on some other software) to produce a low-resolution image, which I then crop with the image box and perform the scan proper into my photo-editor. I then edit the image as required.

Scanned images of Antoninus Pius silver *denarius*.

The same coin photographed with a digital camera.

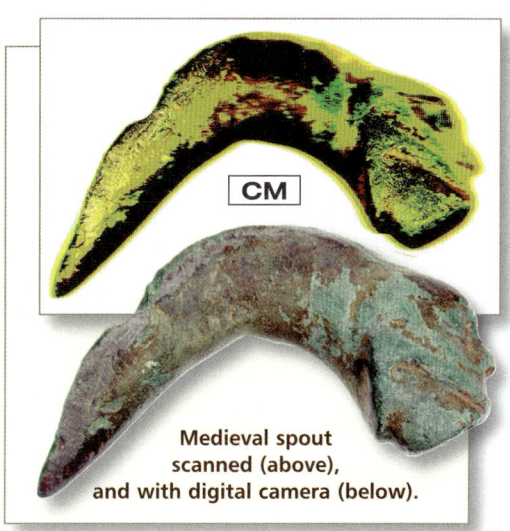

Medieval spout scanned (above), and with digital camera (below).

85

Storage & Display

If you read the conservation advice floating around, there are so many materials that should not be used for storing and displaying metal objects you would be forgiven for thinking it would be better just to leave everything in the Dry Box. The advice is given out in good faith from bitter experience, and there are horror stories of curators storing lead objects in solid oak cabinets, for instance, only to find, when they came to examine their collection years later, heaps of dust where the artefacts once were.

Fifteen years ago I made up a display of finds in total naivety using almost as many wrong materials and methods as it was possible to achieve. I used the wrong wood, the wrong foam with the wrong covering, the wrong attachment method and materials, and made no attempt to protect the finds. It's true that the foam disintegrated and some of the objects are tarnished; but all the finds are perfectly sound although most are not in their original position. I may have just been lucky, of course, but one of the big advantages of storage and display systems is that you can easily look at your finds regularly and you will soon notice and deal with any corrosion.

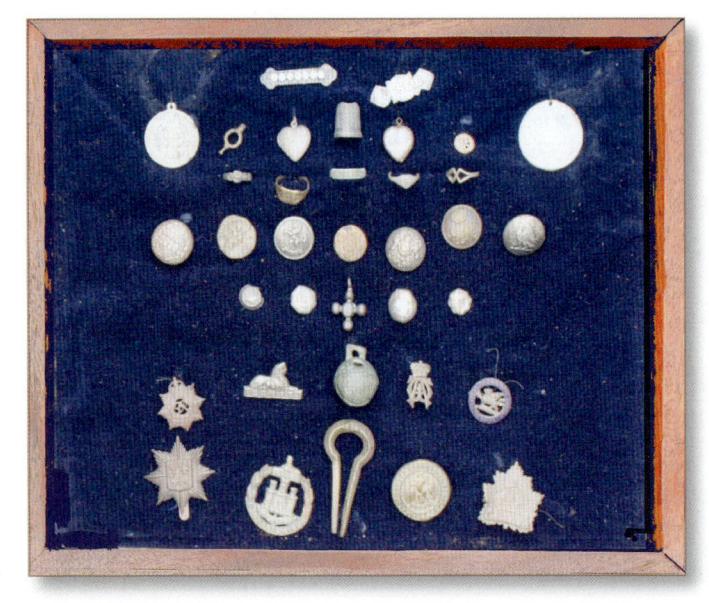

Display case made up 15 years ago.

There is one sure, simple way to protect your finds from the ravages of storage and display, which is to coat them with a conservation grade lacquer (Incralac or Paraloid B72 preferably). Treating objects with Renaissance Wax will also protect them. Another way is to make replicas and display them instead of the actual find. If you protect or replicate your finds you can store or display them in almost any way you like, providing you do nothing that will damage protective coatings.

If you don't want to lacquer your finds then safe storage and display options become more limited, but far from impossible. Clearly any product made for the coin (and similar) collectors' market is going to be perfectly safe for storing finds. Lindner and Safe are the two main quality manufacturers for collectables storage and many metal detector dealers stock their products.

There is almost no entirely satisfactory storage solution that works for both coins and artefacts, so we are really going to need to discuss them separately. Coins, tokens, medals, jettons and similar small slim artefacts benefit from having a large range of storage and display possibilities to choose from. In the range for coins etc there are a number of options starting with wallets and capsules for individual items, or coin albums, trays, boxes, cases and cabinets for multiples. Most systems expand to cater for the growing collection and it may be worth visiting your dealer or sending for catalogues before you choose your system. Coin albums are fairly widely available in stores such as Smiths, Boots, Woolworths etc and the cut-price supermarket chains like Lidl, Aldi and Netto often offer collecting systems at a bargain price, particularly in the run up to Christmas. But remember that you get the quality that you pay for!

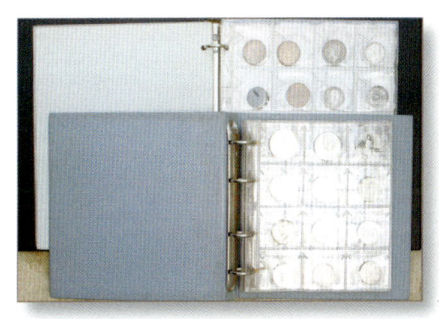

Typical coin albums.

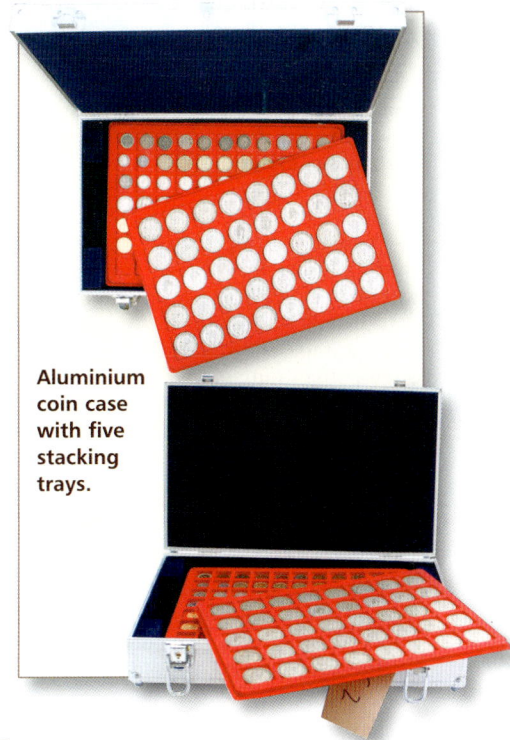

Aluminium coin case with five stacking trays.

for 6, 12, 24 or 45 compartments, and "velvet" inlays for the drawer itself as well as 6, 12 or 24 compartment dividers.

The only slight niggle with the system is that the only coin tray that fits the drawers displays the coins to the side rather than to the end; but I can live with that and these storage units are constantly on my Christmas and birthday wants lists. However, as generous as my friends and family are, I haven't nearly enough of these units to store all my finds so I still need DIY storage, not to mention bespoke displays.

Lindner stacking coin trays.

One style of Safe stackable coin tray, which also fits draws in the universal box storage system.

Safe universal box storage system.

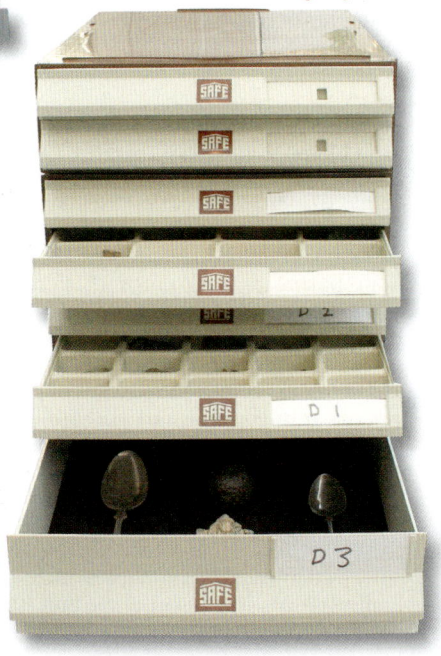

Artefacts come in all shapes and sizes, and for this reason storage that caters for everything is quite rare; many detectorists therefore make up their own storage. Both Lindner and Safe offer a small range of collection or collecting boxes for the smaller finds. For the larger finder, Safe make the universal box storage system, which consists of a drawer unit containing a choice of one or two drawers, 70mm and 33mm high respectively. The units stack vertically and horizontally so you can have floor to ceiling and wall to wall finds storage if you have the finds to go in them. The drawers can be customised by the addition of a drop-in divider

88

Before we move on to the mechanics of DIY storage and display we need to consider the materials we are using.

Adhesives: The only suitable adhesives are acrylics, such as Paraloid B72, or Cellulose Nitrate. Avoid attaching any sticky substance such as Blu-Tack directly to a metal object unless the object is lacquered. Sticky substances will stain the object and may be difficult or impossible to remove.

Boards: Use marine plywood or Medium Density Fibreboard (MDF) - Zero Grade, which both contain reduced formaldehyde resins. These will need to be sealed as for wood below. Avoid chipboard, hardboard, particleboard and plywood as the resins used in construction can produce destructive acids. Glass is inert and stable so it will not normally harm finds; however, it is heavy, breakable and prone to having sharp edges.

Metals: If two dissimilar bare metals come into contact where moisture is present, such as in normal air, an electric current is set up which causes electrolytic corrosion to take place (usually where the metals touch). Providing there is no bare metal touching the objects or they are not lying on textiles or paper, which will hold moisture, aluminium and steel can be used. Metal storage and display units will normally be powder coated or stove enamelled, which is fine. But beware any scratches exposing bare metal, which should either be insulated from finds with a non-metallic waterproof barrier such as Plastazote or Tyvek or the bare metal lacquered. For the same reason, any metal pins used to support objects should either be lacquered or sheathed using polyethylene plastic (ie catheter tubing).

Paper and Card: Use acid-free materials or treat as wood with acrylic varnish. Acid-free paper lined support boards, such as Fome-Cor or Foamex, are available.

Plastics: Polyethylene and acrylic plastics are ideal to use as they are inert and stable. They come with a number of names in a variety of forms including: Perspex, Correx, Tyvek and Plastazote. Avoid Polyvinyl chloride (PVC) plastics, which give off hydrochloric acid and Polystyrene sheet, which yellows with age.

Textiles: Use textiles made from plant fibres such as cotton or linen, preferably un-dyed and unbleached. Synthetics are generally satisfactory too, particularly those produced for collectors. Avoid animal fibres such as wool, including materials containing wool like felt and carpet. Wires, hooks and threads should be avoided. The very small surface area puts pressure on the contact point, which may damage soft metal objects or lacquer but more likely will deteriorate and break, dropping the object.

Wood: All woods are prone to giving off acid vapours but are probably unavoidable in many storage and display applications. Treat all surfaces of wood and composite wood boards with at least three coats of acrylic varnish allowing plenty of time for each coat to thoroughly dry before applying the next. Cuprinol Trade Quick Drying Varnish or Rustin's Quick-Drying Clear Satin Varnish can be used. Make good any screw holes before varnishing and try not to use pins and the like, which will penetrate the varnish and release the wood acids. Avoid oak, unseasoned woods and keeping lead objects in wooden storage or display cases unless the lead is lacquered. Do not use Polyurethane varnish for sealing as this also produces acids.

The amount of finds build up surprisingly quickly and the problem of storing them is perhaps a nice one to have. There will be many run-of-the-mill, buttons, buckles, lead weights, musket balls, furniture fittings and other regular finds, which are too good to scrap but not good enough to earn a place among the cream of finds, (depending on your outlook, of course).

The best way of dealing with these everyday finds is to get hold of a number of 500ml microwaveable plastic dishes with lids; these can be purchased from pound shops or saved from your Chinese take-away meals, if you like. Label the side of each container in permanent marker with the place where the finds within came from: a farm, a field, part of a field; break it down as much as you need to accommodate the finds and save everything that isn't obviously junk in these labelled boxes. A date or a year written on the boxes is a good idea also. To minimise corrosion, make sure the finds are perfectly dry before you put them into the boxes. You'll see the benefit of this system as time goes on when you start recognising Saxon horse harness fittings and pieces of Bronze Age metalwork lying amongst the dross. Also you may be able to match up parts of recently found objects with other parts you found previously.

The next thing, of course, is somewhere to store your growing collection of boxes. You may already have a cupboard or similar but chances are you won't because clutter always expands to fill the space available. A cheap and cheerful way of storing these boxes is in plastic A4 filing draw units, which you can get from stores like Wilkinsons and Woolworths. The one I'm using has six shallow drawers, each holding between four and six 500ml containers, so that's 24-36 containers per unit. When you've filled one unit, just get another and apart from maintaining a regular check every couple of months to ensure there is no corrosion taking place and finding somewhere dry and under cover to stand the units, that's the bulk of the finds storage sorted.

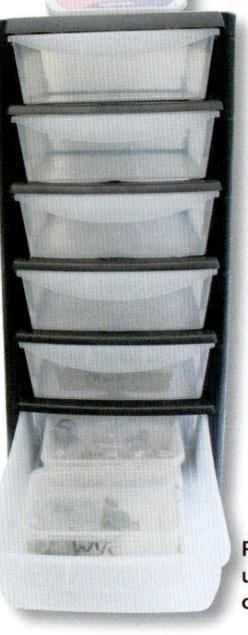

Plastic A4 filing drawer unit with microwaveable containers.

For the better finds some go for the collecting systems already discussed while others carry on with filing drawers but probably push the boat out a bit and go for better quality units made of wood or metal. Line the drawer with a suitable material such as un-dyed, unbleached cotton cloth from a haberdasher and just lay the finds out with a neatly written label (preferably using Tyvek and permanent marker). This is probably not the safest storage method if you have children or dogs running amok, unless you can keep the unit somewhere out of the way.

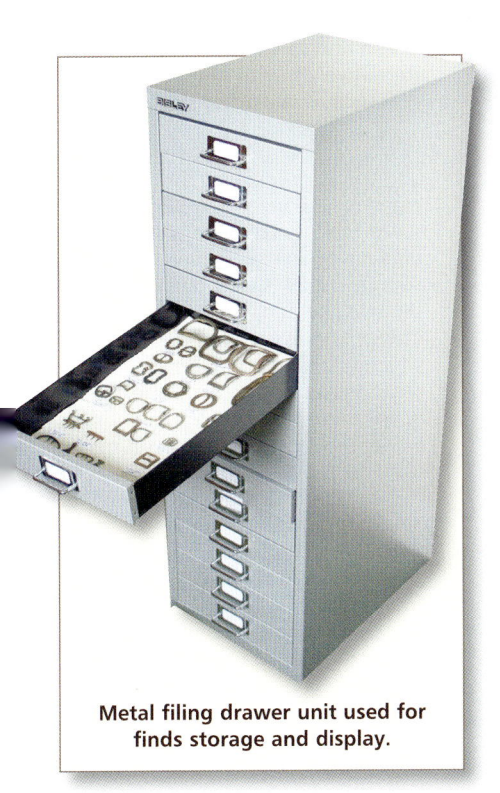

Two items of wooden furniture used for finds storage and display.

Just In Case Company divided display case.

Most collecting systems will double as flat displays perhaps with the addition of a clear Perspex top to keep dust out and finds in! Just In Case Company also manufactures display cases in ranges of divided wood and aluminium. However, if you want permanent or semi-permanent angled or vertical displays a little application is needed. Unfortunately, unless you have very deep pockets it is quite difficult to get hold of display cases that are perfect for the job and even collectors' cases may require some modification.

There are, however, some simple solutions. One is nautical display cases containing knots and models which are mandatory at boot fairs and often found

Metal filing drawer unit used for finds storage and display.

in pound-stretcher type shops. These come in a range of sizes and being deeper than picture frames will suit coins and a good range of artefacts. The frame could even be extended rearwards by adding wooden laths to accommodate most or all artefacts. The back will probably be hardboard or plywood and would be best replaced with a more metal-friendly board. (This may require varnishing and the inside of the wooden frame will need varnishing.)

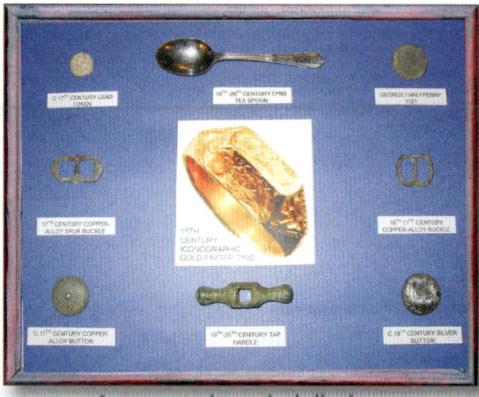

A converted nautical display case. Note: Pictures can be usefully used in displays as here to show a ring, which had become museum property and also to show enlargements or alternative views of objects displayed such as the other side of a coin.

A small commercial display case.

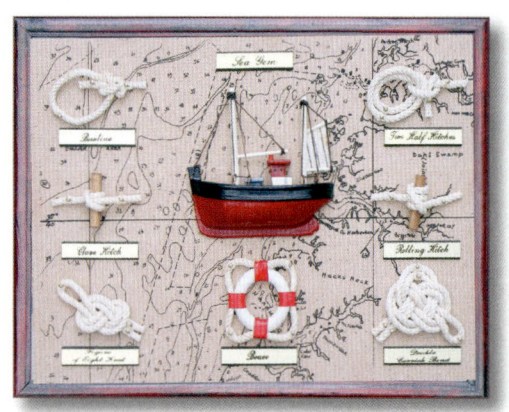

Typical nautical display case that readily lends itself to conversion.

Another possibility for larger displays is to convert a paste table. A paste table is basically two approximately 3 feet x 2 feet, or 1m x 500mm, cases joined by hinges. Just remove the hinges, legs and other fittings to give you your basic cases to which you can fit clear Perspex fronts using either screws and cup washers or mirror corners. Varnish all the wood inside and out and you might want to replace the board that will become the back of the case, as it will be either hardboard or chipboard.

If you want smaller cases you can cut down the tabletops and adjust the side timbers to suit, although if you intend to make significant changes it would be preferable to make a case from scratch, using better materials. If you have the woodworking skills, or know somebody who has, you can make or have made, whatever style of display case you need. The only tricky bit for some of us is the corners which look best mitred or even dovetailed; however, simple butt joints or even corner plates would be quite adequate as the main attraction will be the display of finds.

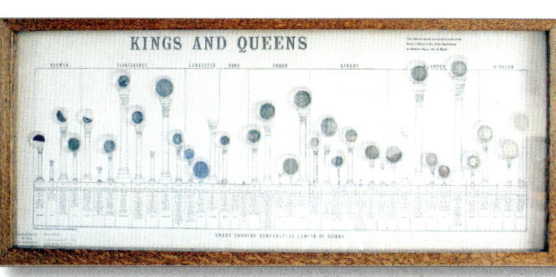

Coins mounted in capsules on a chart. The Kings and Queens chart is © Crown Copyright 1967.

Empty display case made from a paste table top, size 880mm x 560mm.

Mounting finds in vertical or angled display cases against gravity can be tricky unless you lacquer your finds, when you can just fix them in place with Blu-Tack or similar. If you don't lacquer your finds the only inert adhesives are Paraloid B72 or cellulose nitrate, which are neither strong nor easy to use for sticking finds in place. The adhesive can be easily removed with acetone without damaging the object but whatever the object has been attached to, may suffer. If you are going to use this method of fixing a divided display case would be useful as you can support the bottom of the object on dividing ribs and only have to prevent horizontal movement.

A method that lends itself to coins and similar thin objects is to place the object in a coin capsule then mount the capsule with Blu-Tack. Very small coins and fractions can be kept in place by using a suitable packing material such as jiffy foam or acid-free tissue. If you need to remove the capsule from the chart you will do less damage to the chart if you twist the capsule off, rather than pulling it straight off.

The preferred method for un-lacquered objects is to fill the frame up with plastazote sheets, available from conservation suppliers, size 1m x 1.5m in 3mm, 5mm, 9mm, 12mm, 15mm and 30mm thickness in grey (black and white is also available but subject to minimum order quantities).

It is then a matter of cutting out the material to form a void for the object, which will then stay fully supported in position, held against the glass. Before you start I suggest you lay your finds out on paper or similar in the arrangement that you want to achieve. It's not very easy to scoop out material with a blade so I suggest you cut completely through the Plastazote sheet and this would be best done using the minimum

3mm thick sheet and building a suitable thickness up layer by layer. Using a sharp craft knife or scalpel, carefully cut out a sheet to fit snugly against the inside of the frame glass. Use a cutting board or some scrap board beneath the Plastazote as the blade will obviously go through the Plastazote and probably mark whatever is beneath it.

Owing to the unwieldy size of Plastazote sheets it would be prudent to use the outside of the finished frame as a template to cut the first sheet out into a manageable form. With luck you will have a good straight edge in both the vertical and horizontal directions to work from. Then measure in each direction to the glass size, slightly larger rather than smaller, and trim off against a straight edge to get the final size. Save all your reasonable-sized off-cuts as they can be used for packaging finds etc.

Fit the Plastazote against the inside of the glass and mark both the top of the frame and the top of the Plastazote sheet where they won't be seen so you know which way is up. Mark out the Plastazote sheet on the non-display side with a fine felt-tip pen starting from the centre putting in as many lines as you can such as horizontal and vertical centres and top and bottom limits. When you start cutting remember that the first sheet will be the finished face of the display so proceed very, very carefully; there is no rush - your display will last for years. If you do make a mistake you can re-use the sheet further down the stack but obviously it is better to get it right first time. Starting with the central object, or nearest, mark round the object and cut out its shape in the Plastazote. Straight lines are easier than curves and you will probably need to remove the sheet to cut through it completely. From there, work up and down the vertical centre line marking around and cutting out for the other objects, starting with the top and bottom objects and spacing out the others as evenly as possible or to your own design. Once you have cut the voids in the vertical centre line you can mark out the horizontal lines to suit the other objects in the display and then mark out the vertical lines. Having marked the sheet out you can lay the objects face down in position, starting with the centre row and follow on row by row. Bear in mind that you are working from the rear of the frame so the layout will be a mirror image of the finished display.

Rear of the first sheet of Plastazote completed with the objects in place.

Once you have done all that, use the sheet as a template to mark out and cut the next sheet of Plastazote.

Fit that into the frame on top of the first sheet and mark the top. Remove the new sheet, leaving the first sheet in the frame and apply conservation grade adhesive, such as Paraloid B72, fairly liberally over the solid areas of the sheet in the frame. Where you are displaying thin flat objects, which may slide between the Plastazote sheets, apply adhesive on the solid area around the bottom and sides of the object void; however, this can be done later if necessary. Lay the new sheet on top of the first sheet, firm it down with your hands, then lay a heavy book, large enough to cover most of the sheet, on top and leave at least half an hour for the adhesive to set.

Once the adhesive has set remove the Plastazote sandwich and - working from the display side - this time start fitting the objects, face up into the voids cutting out the new sheet below as necessary. You shouldn't mark the cuts with felt-tipped pen this time as ink marks may be left showing from the front but, where the objects are robust, you can gently push down on them, which will mark the Plastazote below and you will see where you need to cut.

Once you have completed all necessary cutting out, just keep adding new sheets onto the stack in the same way, cutting out as necessary, until you have filled the depth of the frame so that the frame back holds the Plastazote sandwich block securely against the glass. As the depth of Plastazote increases and there is less room to manoeuvre the scalpel or knife you may find it easier to make what cuts you can from the front then turn over and finish cutting out from the rear. Also, you can make layers up from off-cuts if you wish to economise on material. With the block removed from the frame, pop your objects into their cavities from the front, slip the frame over the top, fit the back on the frame and you're done.

The completed display.

If you only have a handful of finds you will easily be able to keep track of everything; however, when your finds start numbering in the hundreds and thousands you may benefit from having a database. Finds databases have come and gone in the past but it is fairly simple to construct your own with a modicum of computer experience or you could just produce a paper log along the same lines. I have constructed the following database for my own use on Microsoft Excel, one of the Microsoft Office suite programs. Microsoft Access is the main database software and some people can work wonders with it; unfortunately, I find it user-unfriendly and prefer the relative simplicity of Excel. If you don't have Microsoft Office there is a free alternative, you may want to investigate, available at www.openoffice.org

The database headings should be fairly self-explanatory; however I'll just go through them briefly below.

Date - The date the object was found

Type - The type of object, which may simply be coin or artefact, but it is better if artefacts are broken down into groups like button, buckle, weight, etc.

Description - A suitable description of the object which can be just a few words or an essay, as you wish

Find spot - At least the OS 6-figure grid reference, unless you intend to make the database public, when a lesser figure or non-descript field name would be more appropriate

Location - Where the object is now, in this case T1 refers to coin tray number 1; D3 to drawer number 3

Reference - Where the object has been published or any publication which supports your identification

PAS - If you are reporting to the PAS it is useful to have the number to be able to track your object on their vast database

My database is just a working example that suits me and is far from the be all and end all of databases. Just modify it to suit yourself. You will also find it extremely useful to include images of your finds.

An example of a finds database.

The Treasure Act

At present "treasure" is defined, under the Treasure Act 1996, as any object other than a coin, at least 300 years old when found, which has a metallic content, of which at least 10% by weight is gold or silver. And all coins that contain at least 10% by weight of gold or silver that come from the same find consisting of at least two coins, at least 300 years old. And all coins that contain less than 10% by weight gold or silver that come from the same find consisting of at least 10 coins at least 300 years old. And any associated objects (eg a pot or other container), except unworked natural objects found in the same place as treasure objects. And any objects or coin hoards less than 300 years old, made substantially of gold and silver that have been deliberately hidden with the intention of recovery and for which the owner is unknown.

From 1 January 2003 the definition of treasure has been extended on prehistoric (ie up to the end of the Iron Age) finds to include all multiple artefacts, made of any metal, found together and single artefacts deliberately containing any quantity of precious metal.

The Act applies to objects found anywhere in England, Wales and Northern Ireland, including in or on land, in buildings (whether occupied or ruined), in rivers and lakes and on the foreshore (the area between mean high water and mean low water) providing the object does not come from a wreck. If the object has come from a wreck then it will be subject to the salvage regime that applies to wreck under the Merchant Shipping Act 1995. The Receiver of Wreck (located via Customs & Excise) must legally be notified of all property recovered following the loss of a vessel; and the salvor is entitled to a reward related to the value of the object, either from the owner, if identified, or the Crown.

If you are searching in other parts of the British Isles or outside of Britain altogether, you should familiarise yourself with treasure law for your specific area. In Scotland, for instance, all ownerless objects belong to the Crown. They must be reported regardless of where they were found or of what they are made. The finder receives market value so long as no laws have been broken. Not all finds will be claimed. Further information from: Treasure Trove Unit, National Museums of Scotland, Chambers Street, Edinburgh EH1 1JF.

I have the experience of having had to report seven separate finds of treasure since the introduction of the Treasure Act. There is little wrong with the Treasure Act itself but problems can arise when the Code of Practice isn't followed. My major concern is the lack of confidentiality promised regarding the find spot, for it seems that a number of Coroners, in the early days, gave away fairly precise details of find spots to the Press. For the benefit of novices the implication is that if thieves, usually called "nighthawks", learn the location of your site they may raid it in the hope of finding more treasure and may cause serious damage to the landowner's crops or other property in the process. You wouldn't blame the landowner if he then banned you from his land with his neighbours probably following suit. Painting the blackest picture, you could lose access to vast tracts of land and countless other treasures.

You are probably thinking if that is what could happen when you comply with the law you'll keep quiet when you find treasure. Unfortunately, the penalty for not reporting is far greater for, if you get caught, you may be fined up to £5,000 and be imprisoned for three months. You are then branded a criminal, which could seriously ruin your life.

But things are not as bad as they may look; mostly good things come from your honesty, like access to the next site and your next treasure find. The problems can be overcome if you know how. And you will know how by the time you've finished reading this chapter.

My first treasure find, in February 1999, was a gilt silver medieval ring brooch, unfortunately missing its sword-shaped pin, inscribed with the letters "IESVSX" (Jesus Christ) found in close proximity to two contemporary silver coins. The find spot, on the site of a medieval Hundred Court, was near the boundary between two Coroners' provinces. It took three weeks to get one of them to accept responsibility as the Coroner's Officers were out most of the time and didn't return calls.

I was asked to deposit the find with a choice of three or four fairly local museums. I chose the most convenient to me and I am pleased to say the curator was very helpful. The landowner was on holiday at the time of the find and I arranged to delay depositing the items with the museum until the landowner had the opportunity to view them. When I deposited the objects in April, the curator advised putting a four-figure Ordnance Survey map reference on the Treasure Receipt and recorded the eight-figure reference separately.

The Museum didn't want to acquire the finds and after reference was made to the landowner, they were disclaimed and returned to me without fuss or publicity on 17 September 1999.

The second instance began in April 1999 with the finding of a single Ambiani type E Iron Age gold stater by the landowner. This coin didn't qualify as treasure by itself and wasn't reported. On 30 September 1999, I found two more Ambiani gold staters in the same place and reported all three to the Coroner about 12 days later. (I knew who the Coroner was this time.) Because of the

Silver medieval ring brooch.

difficulties of my getting to a museum (at my own expense), we arranged for the finds to be deposited by the landowner at a different museum to the previous find. Based on advice previously received, I briefed the landowner on what information to put on the Treasure Receipt. With the agreement of the landowner, the curator filled in both the Treasure Receipt and the museum's standard receipt, recording eight-figure find spots together with the name of the farm on both receipts. The landowner was given the museum receipt and we were both later sent copies of the official Treasure Receipt.

During December 1999 and early January 2000, I recovered four more Ambiani staters, one by one from the same place. I reported each one to the Coroner within 14 days of each find and the four were handed over to the museum on 10 January 2000 by the landowner. The dual receipting procedure was repeated although in answer to the landowner's comments about terms on the museum receipt, which couldn't be applied to potential treasure finds, the curator crossed out the disagreeable parts.

The inquest was originally scheduled for late January but was postponed to 24 February as a result of the additional finds. The inquest was a quiet affair with only the landowner, Coroner, two officers and myself in attendance. The coins were inevitably declared "Treasure", the museum having an interest in acquiring them. Expenses were offered for attending court.

The Coroner's officer phoned the following day to tell me that the local Press wanted to speak to me, he also told me that he was legally obliged to reveal details of the find to the Press. I had discussions with the landowner who wanted no publicity. We decided that it would be better to speak to the Press and appeal to them not to reveal sensitive information, rather than risk them making their own stories up from what they

Eight of the staters displayed after being declared treasure and acquired by the museum (with kind permission Museum of Canterbury).

got from the Coroner's office. While one reporter made it clear that he knew the landowner's name and the name of the farm, he did act responsibly and complied with our wishes to publish neither.

The Curator took the coins to the British Museum. We (landowner and myself) then received a letter from the Department for Culture, Media and Sport (who administer the Treasure Act) saying the coins were being valued, the valuation would be sent to us and we would have 28 days to comment and offer alternative valuations. I did actually attempt to obtain a couple of valuations but could only get ballpark figures without the valuers being able to view the actual coins. One dealer requested £50 for this service but subsequently gave me a free retail valuation for which I was grateful.

On 11 May I received a letter from the Department for Culture, Media and Sport with a valuation report from Sotheby's (£1260-£1400). The letter said that the valuation committee was sitting the following day and we were not going to be allowed to make representations on the provisional valuation owing to public holidays.

On 16 May the Department for Culture Media and Sport advised that the committee had valued the coins at £1350 and we had one month to make representation if dissatisfied. The museum was also allowed to make representation on the valuation. The museum then had up to four months to settle, from the time this figure was accepted by all parties. We agreed to accept the valuation, which was close to the ballpark figures given by the dealers.

Discussing this case with Bob Whalley, Co-ordinator for Policy, National Council for Metal Detecting, it came to light that the first coin found by the landowner should not have been declared Treasure as it was only a single find at the time. The Department for Culture, Media and Sport agreed. The museum wanted all seven coins to maintain the integrity of the supposed hoard; however, by request the coin was returned to the landowner and an agreed pro rata award, split equally between the landowner and myself, was made for the other six coins during October 2000.

After the autumn ploughing the landowner and myself found a further Ambiani stater each on the same field. I reported these to the Coroner within the stipulated 14 days and suggested we delayed handing the coins over until I had carried out further searching. As it happened, I didn't find any more coins, so the landowner took the two coins to the museum in mid-January 2001. The museum wanted these coins to add to the other six so they inevitably were going to be declared treasure. I was quite puzzled why the museum even wanted the coins in the first place, as Ambiani staters must be the most common Iron Age gold coins of all. In answer to that question the curator told me that they needed to keep them together for posterity and future research when improved analytical techniques may be able to provide more information.

Between January and the Inquest in May, the Coroner and his two officers all retired leaving a Deputy Coroner and a new officer to take charge of the case. As the Coroner's officer suggested the inquest was going to be just a brief formality, neither the landowner nor myself attended. The following day the Coroner's officer rang the landowner saying that the coins had been declared treasure and the Press had been given details, including the landowner's telephone number. The landowner was not happy and I was not happy; by the following week when a report on the find appeared in the local paper, giving the full name and address of the farm, in the midst of the Foot and Mouth crisis, we were livid. Locally there was not much that could be done other than to ask neighbours to look out for intruders, while Bob Whalley and I moved into written complaint mode. Bob wrote to the Deputy Coroner while I tackled Doctor Roger Bland, Adviser on Treasure. We eventually received replies from Doctor Bland, the Deputy Coroner, and from two other Coroners who had each inherited part of the retired Coroner's area owing to a county reorganisation.

The deputy Coroner said it wasn't anything to do with her any longer and couldn't comment, while one of the "new" Coroners said she only referred to find spots by map reference. The second "new" Coroner, on the other hand, while suggesting that information was given to the Press during the inquest, somewhat more encouragingly confirmed that her officers should not report find spots to the Press and promised to check out other possible sources of "leaks", such as the Police Press Office.

Meanwhile the valuation was set at £440 for the two coins that the Deputy Coroner had determined had both been found by me and my attempts to rectify that verdict have fallen on deaf ears. The landowner and myself accepted the award, which was paid in January 2002, split 75% in favour of the landowner (I couldn't really claim half the value of a coin I didn't find).

In June 2002 on a club search in the grounds of a medieval manor house I found, within 10 minutes, a 15th century iconographic gold finger ring

Gold iconographic finger ring, 15th-16th century.

engraved with figures of Saint Catherine, a bearded male believed to be Saint John the Baptist, and floral motifs. This clearly had to be reported to the Coroner. Aware of the recent reorganisation in the county, I wrote to the most likely candidate from the Treasure Act Code of Practice book and asked that my letter be passed to the appropriate Coroner if that office no longer dealt with the parish where I had found the ring. My letter was passed on to another Coroner who turned out to be the lady who only refers to the find spot by map reference.

I was asked to take the ring to the museum, which had dealt with the staters and we went straight for the Treasure Receipt this time. I only gave a four-figure map reference for the find spot to be entered on the Treasure Receipt even though the Curator wanted six. I explained why I didn't want the full find spot reference recorded on the receipt and offered it to be kept separately although that was declined for the moment. The local museum wanted the ring so it went to Treasure Inquest, which unfortunately was scheduled while I was away on holiday and I was unable to attend. There was only the briefest mention of the ring in the local newspaper, giving only the name of the parish as the find spot and I eventually received a half share in the £3750 award.

Roman silver ring with gold stud.

A year (almost to the day) after finding the medieval ring, I found a Roman silver ring with a gold stud supposedly representing the evil eye to protect the wearer. I reported to the Coroner and deposited it, in exchange for a Treasure Receipt, at a different museum that was more convenient at the time. The ring was disclaimed and returned to me with the landowner's agreement.

My next treasure find was a 6th century gold Saxon pendant, which I reported to the same lady Coroner as the previous two finds. By this time the County Finds Liaison Officer (FLO) had taken over the role of "treasure receiver" as a natural extension of his administration of the Portable Antiquities Scheme, where found objects are voluntary reported for inclusion on a national finds database. I handed over the pendant to the FLO in exchange for a Treasure Receipt. The local museum wished to acquire the find so it went to inquest, which I was able to attend and where the Coroner cautioned me not to give out the find spot in court! The press were present and interviewed me after the short hearing, later publishing a small article. They only revealed the name of the parish, and published a photograph of the pendant that I had supplied. I later received my share of the £1300 award.

My last treasure find to date is a 17th century gold "Memento Mori" ring, unfortunately badly damaged by agricultural machinery. I reported this to the same Coroner as previously and handed it over to the FLO in exchange for a Treasure Receipt. Not surprisingly, it has been disclaimed.

Saxon 6th century gold pendant.

Clearly there has been a vast improvement in the handling of potential treasure in my area over the past few years; however, I still urge you to be cautious when reporting your finds.

Here are my unofficial suggestions for protecting yourself and your landowner friends when you find potential treasure:-

* Leave your treasure "as found" and resist all temptation to clean or restore your find except for the absolute minimum necessary to identify it as possible treasure.

* The National Council for Metal Detecting will willingly advise in the process of reporting treasure and it is well worth involving them from the start when you have possible treasure to report.

* County Finds Liaison Officers (FLOs) are now heavily involved in the treasure process and will also advise and help.

* Your only legal obligation is to report the finding of potential treasure to the Coroner within 14 days of becoming aware that it is possibly treasure.

* Discuss the matter with the landowner as soon as possible.

* Do the reporting yourself. The legal responsibility for reporting rests with the finder and no one will look after your interests as well as you.

* Bear in mind - especially if you want to keep a coin - that the first coin found of a scattered hoard may not be treasure, if it was the only coin found on that occasion and there was sufficient time to sell the coin before the finding of the second coin.

* Report your find to the Coroner in writing within 14 days and keep a copy of the letter. In the first instance only report the find spot as the name of the parish in which the find was made. If it is not clear which Coroner needs to be informed, ask your FLO or write to the most likely Coroner and ask for your letter to be passed on, as necessary.

* Always take photographs or have photographs taken of all possible views of all objects, before you hand the objects over. You will at least have something to show an independent valuer and, if you want to publish, there won't be any copyright or access issues.

* There is no time limit for handing over the find and you should be allowed a reasonable amount of time for such things as photographing, valuing, showing it to the landowner, displaying it at a club meeting etc. Bear in mind, however, that you are responsible for the security of the find until you hand it over.

* You will probably be asked to hand your find over to a museum or the county Finds Liaison Officer, at your own expense. If you can arrange this without too much inconvenience then in the interest of good relationships it is best to comply. However, you are under no legal obligation to take your find anywhere and perfectly within your rights to politely suggest the Coroner arrange collection from you. These days FLOs often collect treasure objects from finders anyway.

* Insist on being given the Treasure Receipt (filled out in your presence) in exchange for your find.

* The Treasure Act Code of Practice requires that the precise find spot must be established and should be kept confidential. You can insist on the confidentiality requirement when the Treasure Receipt is completed and have the precise find spot kept separately.

* A section of the Treasure Receipt is labelled "Location of find spot". Only

enter vague details of the find spot such as name of Parish, four-figure map reference or a nondescript name for the site such as "Field A".

* If a museum is interested in acquiring the find, a Coroner's Inquest will be arranged. You should be invited to attend the Inquest for which you can claim expenses, and I suggest you should attend if you possibly can - you will at least know who was there and what was said. The press may be there, so be careful not to reveal find spot information if they are.

* Following an Inquest the Press will probably want to speak to you. Whether you speak to them is up to you but you can at least appeal for some confidentiality and perhaps avoid them uncovering, or inventing, more than you would like revealed.

* The final stumbling block is the valuation, which will be given via the Department for Culture, Media and Sport some weeks after the Inquest. You need to know if the valuation given is indeed a "Fair Market Value" so that you can decide whether to accept it. Fair market value is an attempt to arrive at the price you should expect to get if selling your find on the open market and the Treasure Valuation Committee tries to arrive at the "hammer" price without auctioneer's deductions. Pick out a couple of dealers specialising in coins or objects similar to yours from the advertisements in Treasure Hunting. Ask the dealers to give you their buying-in price for your find (you'll probably have to send photographs). I am sure they will oblige for little or no charge (say £5-£10 unless there is a lot of work involved or the treasure is very valuable). You will find that they will only give you a ballpark figure without seeing the actual finds, which

you don't have. If the treasure is very rare it should be possible to arrange viewing for independent appraisal. You should be offered two opportunities to contest the valuation, one before the valuation committee meets and one after. I would accept the valuation if it falls within or above your dealers' ballpark figures and contest it if it falls below. If you are going to contest the valuation, get in before the committee meets if you can. There is a slight possibility that the museum involved may contest the valuation and succeed in getting it reduced - if this happens, unless there is clear justification, you could appeal against it all the way to the Secretary of State, if necessary.

* An alternative, if both you and the landowner agree, is to refuse any award for the find when you first report it, which will result in the find being disclaimed without inquest and valuation. You are unlikely to have the find returned as it will probably be taken by a museum.

Official Treasure Receipt

There are now two versions of the Treasure Receipt but the content is virtually identical and most importantly both are headed Treasure Act 1996. The actual form can be downloaded from the Cultural Property page at: www.culture.gov.uk

Treasure Trove Assessment Scotland

The form for the reporting of finds for Treasure Trove assessment can be downloaded from the web site www.treasuretrove.org.uk

Department for Culture, Media and Sport

Treasure Act 1996

Receipt for object(s) of potential treasure reported to the coroner

(Copies to be given to the depositor, the coroner and any body to which the object(s) are transferred. If the coroner has already been notified, please attach a copy of his acknowledgement. The SMR should also be informed of the find as soon as possible. The information concerning the findspot should normally be regarded as confidential.)   Reference no:

Institution receiving find:	
Name of person receiving find:	Tel:
Signature:	Date:
Name of person examining find (if different):	Tel:

Signature of depositor: Date:

I confirm that the information given below concerning my name and address and the location, date and circumstances of the find is correct.

Reported to HM Coroner for the District of:

Finder (1)   Name:
Address:
Tel:

Finder (2)   Name:
Address:
Tel:

(N.B. If there are more than two finders their names, addresses and telephone numbers should be noted separately. If the objects found by the different finders are to be kept separate, it might be better to fill out a separate form for each finder.)

Occupier of land   Name:
Address:
Tel:

Owner of land
(if known and if different from the occupier)
Name:
Address:
Tel:

Date of find:

Page 1

Official Treasure Receipt (first page).

Circumstances of find:

(For example: depth of the find; whether on cultivated land or grassland; whether other objects, such as metal or pottery fragments or building rubble, have been found nearby. Continue on a separate sheet if necessary.)

Location of findspot:

(At least a six figure grid reference, along with the parish and county. A map may be attached. Since this information will be confidential, it may be advisable to keep a separate record of it.)

To be known as:

Brief description of object(s):

(For example: object type and material; inscriptions or decoration; weight and dimensions; condition. A photograph may be included. Continue on a separate sheet if necessary.)

No. of items deposited:

Subsequent action – Subsequent transfers of the object(s) should be noted below

Institution receiving find:

Name of person receiving find: Tel:

Signature: Date:

Name of person examining find (if different):   Tel:

If object(s) are considered to be treasure, once the coroner has been informed, the British Museum/National Museums & Galleries of Wales should be notified.

Date of notification of British Museum/ National Museums & Galleries of Wales:

If object(s) are not considered to be treasure, the coroner should be informed and authorisation sought to return the object(s):

Date of notification of coroner:

Date authorisation received from coroner:

Date of return of object(s):

Signature of recipient:

To download extra copies of this form, please visit the Cultural Property page at www.culture.gov.uk

Page 2

Official Treasure Receipt (second page).

REPORTING OF FINDS FOR TREASURE TROVE ASSESSMENT

Finder's name:..

Address:..

Town:.................................Postcode:............................

County/Region:.................................Tel:.............................

Description of object found:...
(eg harness pendant, axehead, brooch, etc)
....

Findspot of object
(Findspot:...Town:village:............................

County/region:...........................NGR (2 letters 6 figures)........................

Other information you consider to be of relevance
(eg: previous finds made from this area, current and previous use of land, local land-names, local history etc)
....
....

Discovered by metal-detecting   please tick

Discovered by chance   please tick
(eg whilst walking, ploughing, etc)
Being declared for other reasons   please tick
(eg house clearance)

DECLARATION:
I confirm that I am the finder of the object(s) declared above please tick

I have permission to remove the above finds from the findspot please tick

Signature:...Name:............................

Return to:
TREASURE TROVE SECRETARIAT, NATIONAL MUSEUMS OF SCOTLAND, CHAMBERS STREET, EDINBURGH EH1 1JF
Tel:0131-247-4082/4355 Fax: 0131-247-4060 email:info@treasuretrove.org.uk
Email: HYPERLINK "mailto:info@treasuretrove.org.co.uk" info@treasuretrove.org.uk   www.treasuretrove.org.uk

Form for reporting of finds for Treasure Trove Assessment (Scotland).

Bibliography & Sources

Alec Tiranti Limited **The Silicone Rubber Booklet** (2003).

Collections Trust **Collections Link** (http://www.collectionslink.org.uk).

Cronyn, J.M., **The Elements of Archaeological Conservation** (Routledge, 1990).

Cuddeford, Michael J. **Cleaning and Restoring Coins and Artefacts** (Chelmsford, 1995).

Department for Culture, Media and Sport **The Treasure Act 1996, Code of Practice (Revised) England and Wales** (DCMS, 2002).

Finney Libby, **Basic Conservation and Environmental Monitoring** (Association of Independent Museums, 2006).

Hardy, R. Allen, **The Jewelry Repair Manual** (New York, 1996).

HM Revenue and Customs **Production, distribution and use of denatured alcohol** (HMRC Reference: Notice 473, July 2005).

Hobbs, Richard, Honeycombe Celia, Watkins, Sarah **Guide to Conservation for Metal Detectorists** (Tempus Publishing, 2002).

Hughes, Richard and Rowe, Michael, **The Colouring, Bronzing and Patination of Metals** (Thames & Hudson, 2006).

The Physical and Theoretical Chemistry Laboratory Oxford University **Chemical and Other Safety Information** (http://msds.chem.ox.ac.uk).

Plenderleith, H.J. and Werner A.E.A. **The Conservation of Antiquities and Works of Art** (OUP, 1971).

Portable Antiquities Scheme **Conservation Advice Notes** (MLA, 2005); (http://www.finds.org.uk).

Pulley, Steve **Partefact Restoration for Beginners** (Ipswich, 1998).

Sandes, Kevin R, **The Art of Cleaning Ancient Coins** (http://www.nobleromancoins.com/).

UK Detector Finds Database (http://www.ukdfd.co.uk/)

Villanueva, David **Site Research for Detectorists, Fieldwalkers & Archaeologists** (Greenlight Publishing, 2006).

Watkinson, David, Ed. **First Aid for Finds** (RESCUE/UKIC Archaeological Section, 1981).

Wiltshire County Council Conservation Service **Signposts Factsheet 2: Materials for Storage and Display** (South West Museums, Libraries and Archives Council, 2006).

Suppliers

I have been able to purchase every commercial product mentioned in this book in reasonable quantities at reasonable prices without too much difficulty. However, the book covers a wide range of products and, unfortunately, there is no single supplier for everything mentioned; therefore some shopping around will be needed. Sources of products available locally in supermarkets, chemists, hardware stores, etc, have been mentioned throughout the book and much will be available from metal detecting hobby suppliers, who will be found advertising in **Treasure Hunting** magazine and who deserve our support. I have listed some specialist suppliers below for less easy to obtain products but bear in mind that there may be minimum order quantities or value, and high carriage charges with some of these. A joint purchase through a club or with friends, might be the most cost effective method of acquisition. While I won't be thanked for mentioning Ebay (http://www.ebay.co.uk) in some quarters, I have found the auction site useful in avoiding minimum order quantities (where elsewhere a lifetime's supply is the norm) and for obtaining a few difficult to find products.

Alec Tiranti Ltd 3 Pipers Court, Berkshire Drive, Thatcham, Berkshire, RG19 4ER. Tel. 0845 123 2100 http://www.tiranti.co.uk/ (Modelling and casting equipment, dental picks, scalpels, etc).

Altec Products Ltd Bude Business Centre, Bude EX23 8QN. Tel. 0845 359 9000 http://www.altecweb.com (Wash bottles, laboratory supplies).

Azpack Limited Unit 12 Kernan Drive, Swingbridge Trading Estate, Loughborough, Leicestershire, LE11 5JF. Tel. 01509 261256 http://www.azpack.co.uk (High grade plastic boxes).

Conservation by Design Ltd Timecare Works, 5 Singer Way, Woburn Road Industrial Estate, Kempston, Bedford, MK42 7AW. Tel. 01234 846300 http://www.conservation-by-design.co.uk (Conservation Supplies: Plastazote, Tyvek, etc).

Jessops Jessop House, Scudamore road, Leicester, LE3 1TZ. Tel. 0800 083 3113 http://www.jessops.com (Photographic Supplies).

Just In Case Co The Work Shop, North View, Black Hill, Consett, County Durham, DH8 0JN. Tel. 01207 50 51 53 http://www.just-in-case.biz (Storage and Display).

Lindner Publications 13 Fore Street, Hayle, Cornwall, TR27 4DX. Tel. 01736 751914 http://www.stampaccessories.net (Storage and Display).

Maplin Electronics Ltd Brookfields Way, Manvers, Wath-upon-Dearne, Rotherham, South Yorkshire, S63 5DL. Tel. 0870 4296000 http://www.maplin.co.uk (Electronics)

Museum Reproductions 52 Stonehills Lane, Runcorn, Cheshire, WA5 5UL. Tel. 01928 566689 http://www.museumreproductions.co.uk (Replicas)

Quicktest PO Box 180, Watford, WD19 5JD. Tel. 01923 220206 http://www.quicktest.co.uk (Jewellery Trade Supplies, Magnifiers, Balances)

R & D Laboratories Ltd Unit U, Enkalon Industrial Estate, Antrim, Co. Antrim, BT41 4LJ, Northern Ireland. Tel. 02894465753 http://www.mistralni.co.uk (Chemicals)

Safe Albums (UK) Ltd 16 Falcon Business Park, Hogwood Lane Industrial Estate, Finchampstead, Berkshire, RG40 4QQ. Tel. 0118 9328976 http://www.safealbums.co.uk (Storage and Display)

Sylmasta Ltd PO Box 262, Haywards Heath, West Sussex, RH16 2FR. Tel. 01444 415 027 http://www.sylmasta.com (Restoration Supplies: Paraloid B72)

UKGE Ltd Unit 10 Fountain Way, Reydon Business Park, Reydon, Southwold, Suffolk, IP18 6SZ. Tel. 0800 0336002 http://www.ukge.co.uk (Geologists Equipment: Where-wolf)

Viking Direct PO Box 187, Leicester, LE5 1ZZ. Tel. 0844 4120000 http://www.viking-direct.co.uk (Stationery Supplies, Polythene Bags & Markers)

If all else fails and you can't find a product I've mentioned, by all means contact me at True Treasure Books, 43 Sandpiper Road, Whitstable, Kent, CT5 4DP. Tel 01227 274801, http://www.truetreasurebooks.com and I will endeavour to find you a supplier.

By The Same Author

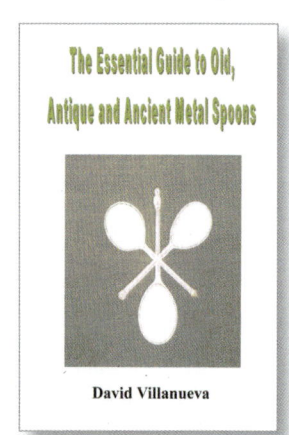

This is a profusely illustrated guide to spoons for finders, collectors, family historians and anyone interested in spoons from earliest times to the 19th century. The book is basically divided into three sections: the first covers the development of spoons, particularly silver, from earliest times; the second covers old base metal spoons and the third, some continental spoons, many of which have been found in Britain. Whatever old spoon you may come across or want information on, you should find it in this book.
Soft Cover, 210mm x 146mm, 88 pages.
ISBN 978-0-9550325-4-7   £4.97 Post Free

By The Same Author

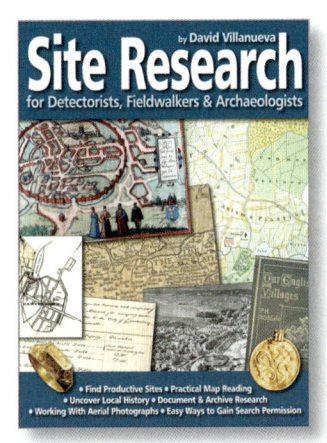

Site Research by David Villanueva — for Detectorists, Fieldwalkers & Archaeologists

Why should one field be productive of finds year after year and yet the next field be totally barren? The answer is past human activity, and this book shows through map and document research, how to locate such activity. Profusely illustrated with examples of maps and documents, and finds resulting from the suggested research methods. Although written mainly for detectorists, this book will also be of interest and help to fieldwalkers, local historians and archaeologists. David Villanueva has over 30 years of experience in metal detecting and research and has been responsible for seven reported finds of Treasure. Using this book you will start to acquire more productive sites and as a result start to make better finds. **Chapter titles:**
● Using Archives, Libraries & Computers ● County Maps ● Ordnance Survey Maps ● Practical Map Reading ● Town Plans ● Road Maps ● Road, River, Canal & Railway Construction Maps ● Enclosure & Tithe Maps ● Estate Maps ● Sea Charts ● Aerial Photographs, Maps & Surveys ● Local Histories ● Guide to County Histories ● Domesday Book ● Gaining Search Permission ● Search Agreements ● Living with the Treasure Act ● Code of Practice ● Bibliography & Sources
250mm x 190mm, 160 pages, £20.00 ISBN 978 1 897738 283

Successful Detecting Sites by David Villanueva contains over 2450 UK site entries. Using rare 18th & 19th century sources, David Villanueva has drawn on over 30 years experience in metal detecting and historical research to compile this exciting guide to thousands of potentially successful detecting sites throughout the United Kingdom, with histories stretching back hundreds or even thousands of years. He explains clearly how to generate a host of successful detecting sites from every place in the guide, which will keep your finds bag overflowing for years to come. And to lead you to these Sites, there is a wealth of valuable information included together with superb facsimiles of 92 highly detailed Victorian maps covering every UK county so you get a complete antique county atlas as well. **Contents:** History of Markets and Fairs in Britain ● The Siting of Markets and Fairs ● Finds from Market and Fair Sites ● Finds from the Routes ● Open-Air Political Meetings ● The Siting of Meeting Places ● Finds from a Hundred Court Site ● Practical Map Reading ● Finding the Sites ● County Atlas and Site Guide for England and Wales ● County Atlas and Site Guide for Scotland ● County Atlas and Site Guide for Northern Ireland & Offshore Islands ● Gaining Search Permission – The Project Approach ● Bibliography and Sources ● Code of Practice
250mm x 190mm, 238 pages, £20.00 ISBN 978 1 897738 306

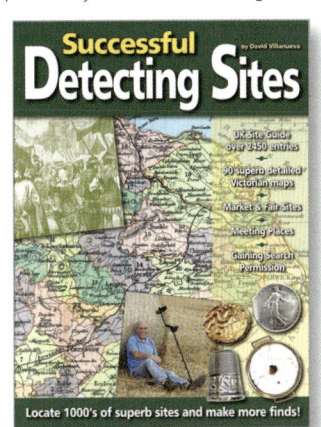

www.greenlightpublishing.co.uk   orders 01376 521900

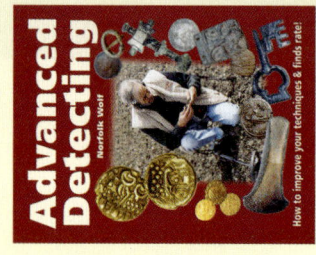

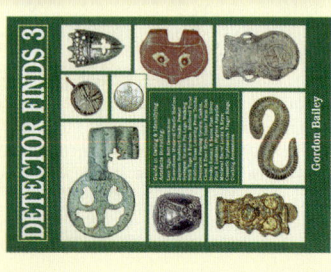

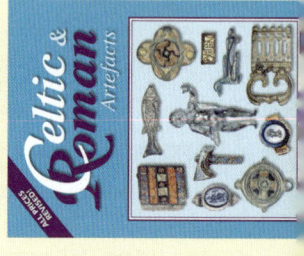

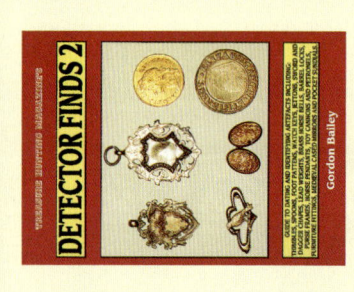

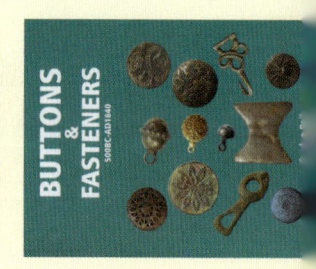

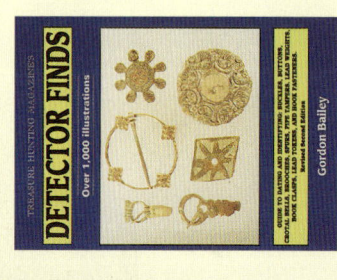

www.greenlightpublishing.co.uk orders 01376 52190

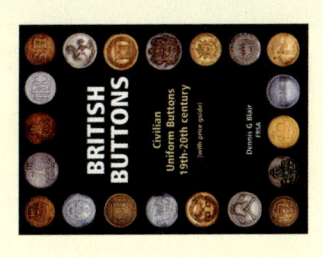

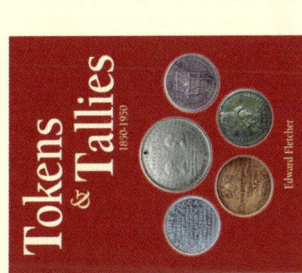

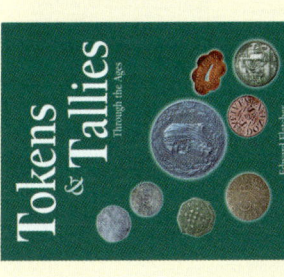

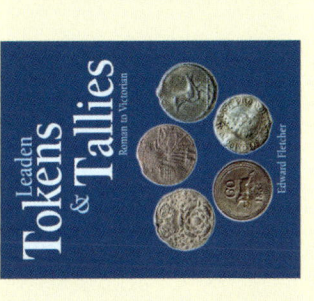

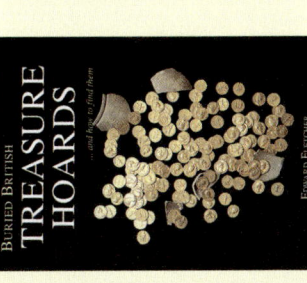

www.greenlightpublishing.co.uk   orders 01376 521900

Treasure hunting

Britain's Best Selling Metal Detecting Magazine

Treasure Hunting is Britain's best-selling metal detecting magazine. Each issue is packed with useful information to help you get the most out of this fascinating hobby.

Content ranges from detector field tests, new product reports, artefact and coin identification guides, site research, detecting techniques to reports on experienced detectorists' finds.

There are regular features like Readers' Letters, News & Views, Questions & Answers, Bookshelf and Club Round-up that help you keep up to date with all the latest happenings in the hobby.

Available at good newsagents, detector retailers or www.greenlightpublishing.co.uk ☎ orders 01376 521900